A–Z
of
Health Foods

A-Z of Health Foods

Carol Bowen

Hamlyn
London · New York · Sydney · Toronto

The author and publishers would like to thank the following for their help in sponsoring photographs for this book:

Batchelor's Foods Limited page 86

Bulmer's Special Reserve Medium Sweet Cider page 103

Carmel Fruit and Vegetables pages 19 and 85

Gale's Honey half title page

Photography by Paul Williams (title page by Robert Golden; page 85 by Carmel Fruit and Vegetables)

Line illustrations by Joyce Tuhill

Published by
The Hamlyn Publishing Group Limited
London · New York · Sydney · Toronto
Astronaut House, Feltham, Middlesex, England
© Copyright
The Hamlyn Publishing Group Limited 1979

ISBN 0 600 34594 7

Phototypeset by Keyspools Ltd, Golborne, Lancashire
Printed in Hong Kong

Contents

Useful Facts and Figures

Notes on metrication

In this book quantities are given in metric and Imperial measures. Exact conversion from Imperial to metric measures does not usually give very convenient working quantities and so the metric measures have been rounded off into units of 25 grams. The table below shows the recommended equivalents.

Ounces	Approx g to nearest whole figure	Recommended conversion to nearest unit of 25	Ounces	Approx g to nearest whole figure	Recommended conversion to nearest unit of 25
1	28	25	11	312	300
2	57	50	12	340	350
3	85	75	13	368	375
4	113	100	14	396	400
5	142	150	15	425	425
6	170	175	16 (1 lb)	454	450
7	198	200	17	482	475
8	227	225	18	510	500
9	255	250	19	539	550
10	283	275	20 (1¼ lb)	0567	575

Note When converting quantities over 20 oz first add the appropriate figures in the centre column, then adjust to the nearest unit of 25. As a general guide, 1 kg (1000 g) equals 2·2 lb or about 2 lb 3 oz. This method of conversion gives good results in nearly all cases, although in certain pastry and cake recipes a more accurate conversion is necessary to produce a balanced recipe.

Liquid measures The millilitre has been used in this book and the following table gives a few examples.

Imperial	Approx ml to nearest whole figure	Recommended ml	Imperial	Approx ml to nearest whole figure	Recommended ml
¼ pint	142	150 ml	1 pint	567	600 ml
½ pint	283	300 ml	1½ pints	851	900 ml
¾ pint	425	450 ml	1¾ pints	992	1000 ml (1 litre)

Spoon measures All spoon measures given in this book are level unless otherwise stated.

Can sizes At present, cans are marked with the exact (usually to the nearest whole number) metric equivalent of the Imperial weight of the contents, so we have followed this practice when giving can sizes.

Oven temperatures

The table below gives recommended equivalents.

	°C	°F	Gas Mark		°C	°F	Gas Mark
Very cool	110	225	$\frac{1}{4}$	Moderately hot	190	375	5
	120	250	$\frac{1}{2}$		200	400	6
Cool	140	275	1	Hot	220	425	7
	150	300	2		230	450	8
Moderate	160	325	3	Very hot	240	475	9
	180	350	4				

Notes for American and Australian users

In America the 8-oz measuring cup is used. In Australia metric measures are now used in conjunction with the standard 250-ml measuring cup. The Imperial pint, used in Britain and Australia, is 20 fl oz, while the American pint is 16 fl oz. It is important to remember that the Australian tablespoon differs from both the British and American tablespoons; the table below gives a comparison. The British standard tablespoon, which has been used throughout this book, holds 17·7 ml, the American 14·2 ml, and the Australian 20 ml. A teaspoon holds approximately 5 ml in all three countries.

British	American	Australian	British	American	Australian
1 teaspoon	1 teaspoon	1 teaspoon	3½ table-spoons	4 table-spoons	3 table-spoons
1 table-spoon	1 table-spoon	1 table-spoon	4 table-spoons	5 table-spoons	3½ table-spoons
2 table-spoons	3 table-spoons	2 table-spoons			

An Imperial/American guide to solid and liquid measures

Imperial	American	Imperial	American
Solid measures		**Liquid measures**	
1 lb butter or margarine	2 cups	¼ pint liquid	⅔ cup liquid
		½ pint	1¼ cups
1 lb flour	4 cups	¾ pint	2 cups
1 lb granulated or castor sugar	2 cups	1 pint	2½ cups
		1½ pints	3¾ cups
1 lb icing sugar	3 cups	1¾ pints	4¼ cups
8 oz rice	1 cup	2 pints	5 cups (2½ pints)

Note When making any of the recipes in this book, only follow one set of measures as they are not interchangeable.

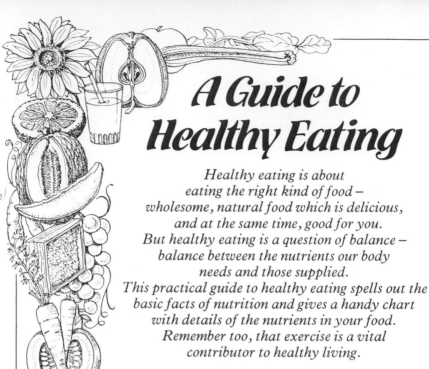

A Guide to Healthy Eating

*Healthy eating is about
eating the right kind of food –
wholesome, natural food which is delicious,
and at the same time, good for you.
But healthy eating is a question of balance –
balance between the nutrients our body
needs and those supplied.
This practical guide to healthy eating spells out the
basic facts of nutrition and gives a handy chart
with details of the nutrients in your food.
Remember too, that exercise is a vital
contributor to healthy living.*

The Balanced Diet

Eating is one of the great pleasures of life. It is not just a source of pleasure, however, because life itself depends upon it. The food we eat greatly affects how we feel, so it is wise to discover what constitutes a healthy diet.

We eat food, but our bodies absorb nutrients. Therefore, to help us to decide what to eat, we must know what nutrients our food contains.

Our diet contains carbohydrates, fats, proteins, minerals and vitamins, plus water and fibre or roughage. Each has a role to play, separately or in co-operation with another.

Carbohydrates and fats are the body's main sources of energy. The role of proteins, minerals and vitamins is in body building and maintenance. Proteins can also provide energy. Fibre is needed for the efficient functioning of the digestive system, while water is necessary for all the body's functions. See the easy guide opposite for an at-a-glance overall picture.

8

Nutrient Chart

Nutrient	Use to the body	Found in
Proteins	Used for maintenance and repair of body tissue, healthy skin, hair, blood and muscles.	Meat, poultry, fish, eggs, cheese, milk, yogurt, nuts, beans and wheatgerm.
Fats	Concentrated source of energy, required for the absorption of fat-soluble vitamins.	Butter, margarine, cream, oily fish, vegetable oils, egg yolk, nuts, fatty meats and cheese.
Carbohydrates	Used to give energy.	Sugars, treacle, molasses, honey, fruit and vegetables, dried fruit, bread, flour, cereals and pulses.
Vitamin A	Protects lining of the respiratory tract, throat and bronchial tubes, eyes and skin. Helps resistance to infection, and gives healthy skin, hair and nails.	Liver, butter, margarine, parsley, carrots, spinach, watercress, salad vegetables, apricots, milk, eggs, cheese, oily fish, fish liver oils, heart and kidney.
Vitamin B Complex	Essential for the utilisation of carbohydrates. Helps give sound nerves, healthy eyes and hair, and resistance to fatigue.	Yeast, yeast extracts, molasses, whole grains, wholemeal bread, brown rice, yogurt, soya beans, peanuts, pork, fish, kidney and liver.
Vitamin C	Maintains the strength of blood vessels and increases resistance to infection. Needed for healthy healing of wounds and for absorption of iron.	Rose-hips, citrus fruits, blackcurrants, salads, green vegetables, green peppers and potatoes.
Vitamin D	Forms strong bones and teeth, aids absorption of calcium.	Butter, margarine, milk, cream, egg yolks, fish liver oil and cod's roe.
Vitamin E	Helps normal growth and development.	Vegetable and nut oils, wheat germ, whole grains, wholemeal bread and eggs.
Vitamin K	Essential for normal clotting of the blood.	Green vegetables such as curly kale, green cabbage and spinach.

Calcium	Aids proper development and the maintenance of bones and teeth. Promotes normal clotting of blood and functioning of muscles.	Milk, cheese, eggs, green vegetables, wholemeal bread and potatoes.
Phosphorus	Together with calcium, forms the hard structure of bones and teeth. Involved in reproduction and transfer of hereditary traits.	Fish, meat, molasses, eggs, green vegetables, cheese, milk, nuts, oranges and dried apricots.
Iron and Copper	Helps build healthy blood cells and resistance to fatigue.	Meat, eggs, molasses, green vegetables, dried apricots, whole grains and pulses.
Magnesium	Essential for correct nerve functioning and the formation of bones and teeth. Helps functioning of glands.	Cereals and vegetables.
Sodium	Maintains the salt concentration of the blood and controls nerve impulse conductors.	Cereals, butter, eggs, milk and cheese.
Potassium	Develops muscle cells and blood corpuscles.	Most common foods, especially vegetables.
Zinc	Essential for health of skin and sexual functions. Required for growth and wound healing.	Wheat, bran, kelp, shellfish and animal protein.

Having digested the basic facts of nutrition and diet, the next step is to use this knowledge to make meals that you will enjoy and from which you will benefit. If nutrition were a perfect science it might be possible to advocate the ideal diet, but since it does not account for personal likes and dislikes, it would not work. There are, however, certain guidelines to be followed to achieve a balanced diet.

The first balance which has to be achieved in a diet is between the energy your food provides and the energy your body uses up. The reason why people become fat is that they eat carbohydrates, fats and proteins in excess of their body's needs, and these are turned into fat.

The average man is reckoned to have an energy output of 3,000 calories per day and a woman 2,200 calories per day.

Fats, proteins and carbohydrates are our sources of energy. But fats and proteins have nutritional roles which carbohydrates cannot fulfil, so a diet must have a balance between the three major nutrients. Proteins are essential for body maintenance, but to consume more than is needed is pointless, as excess protein is converted into fat.

The amount of protein required each day varies considerably with age. It reaches a peak during the teens, drops marginally with adulthood and decreases in old age. The estimated figure for an adult man's daily intake of protein is nearly 85 g (3 oz) in the United Kingdom. A simple rule of thumb for ensuring an adequate supply of protein is to reckon it is about one-tenth of the total energy intake. Thus if you need 3,000 calories a day, proteins should provide 300 calories – that is is nearly 85 g (3 oz) at 110 calories an ounce.

But some proteins, depending on the relative amounts of essential amino acids they contain, are more nutritionally valuable than others. A balance of amino acids is needed in a healthy diet. Wheat, for example, is low in the amino acid lysine, but this can be made good by combining it with such lysine-rich foods as cheese or beans. A diet should be varied to ensure an adequate intake of amino acids.

In the West we eat too much fat. Nutritionists generally agree that fats should contribute between 30 and 40% of our energy intake. In Britain the proportion has reached over 40%. Fortunately we are beginning to eat more vegetable fats than animal fats. This means that the diet is less likely to be short of one of the essential fatty acids, linoleic acid, which is low in most visible animal fats but high in vegetable fats.

No diet is balanced unless it has an adequate supply of minerals and vitamins. In the main, if we balance our diet by eating a wide range of carbohydrates and proteins plus a discriminating choice of fats, we need not worry about consuming enough minerals and vitamins. What we do have to guard against is that we do not, by careless preparation and cooking, destroy too many of these precious vitamins and minerals.

The final balance which has to be achieved is that between eating what we like and what is best for us. The solution is to try to make them the same thing.

Breathe in-Breathe out

Just as important as the food we eat is the exercise we give our bodies. Regular exercise, kept within the body's own capabilities, works wonders for our health, fitness and appearance. By assisting the circulation, exercise helps the flow of oxygen to the muscles, making the skin healthy and glowing and making the whole body more supple.

In order to benefit from exercise you need to adhere to a regular daily routine. Sudden sharp bursts of strenuous physical exercise not only do nothing towards fitness or health, but are very likely to cause muscle strain and fatigue, as the body is unprepared to take the unaccustomed stress.

The amount of exercise the body can take will increase with regular and methodical routine, and, although exercise alone is unlikely to reduce body weight, excess inches can be lost over a period of time by toning and tightening the muscles.

Start with the suggested series of six movements. To begin with, take five minutes a day over the routine, moving to music if you like to keep to a rhythm. As the body grows fitter and can take more strain, increase the exercises, taking up to fifteen minutes.

Try to take some sort of exercise every day. There are plenty of different ways to maintain fitness – any sport or informal exercise such as walking, jogging or swimming contributes greatly to the general health and vitality, leading to a better appearance and complexion.

Leg Stretch
Sit straight, toes pointed. Slowly reach for one foot with both hands, legs as straight as possible. Lower head towards knee. Repeat 3 times each side.

Hip Twist
Lie flat, one leg bent, one straight, arms out to sides. Keep one leg straight. Twist bent knee over body to the ground. Repeat to the other side. Repeat 10 times in all.

Stomach Exercise
Lie flat, arms at sides. Bend knees back towards body, still lying flat. Extend legs in the air. Lower slowly. Repeat 8 times.

Beauty–is it really only skin deep?

Not surprisingly, our choice of food – be it wise or unwise – has a direct bearing on our appearance. Everyone knows that, for most of us, if we eat too much we put on weight, and it therefore probably follows that an improved diet may lead to a clear complexion, a good natural colour, springy step and shiny hair.

Sometimes our appearance suffers because we eat carelessly. Highly refined, starchy foods – the danger foods – are often to blame because, being the least expensive, they are often used to bulk out meals.

To achieve a better, nutritionally balanced diet, seek out fresh fruit and vegetables, packed with vitamins and full of goodness, crusty brown bread, golden honey, whole grain cereals and unspoilt foods, in as near a natural state as possible.

The best way to ensure that you are getting a properly balanced diet, is to base your eating on whole foods, particularly those which contain roughage, such as whole grain cereals, nuts and pulses, together with plenty of fresh fruit and vegetables and the minimum of sugar and fat.

For people who are used to refined foods, this type of diet may seem strange at first. It is, perhaps, advisable to start gradually at first. The recipes which follow will help to get you started. Once you have tasted the full, fresh flavours and experienced the increased health, beauty and vitality which comes from natural foods, you'll never look back!

*Waist Stretch
Stand straight, arms curved over head. Without stooping, bend to one side from the waist. Repeat on the other side. Repeat 10 times.*

*Yoga Cat
Kneel with hands below shoulders. Arch back in, pushing head back. Hold to a count of 5. Hump back, head forward. Hold to a count of 5. Repeat 5 times.*

*Leg Swing
Stand, arms out to sides. Swing right leg forward, toe pointed. Swing leg back, still standing straight. Repeat with foot flexed. Change to left leg. Repeat 5 times.*

13

A-Z of Health Foods

*Not surprisingly,
anyone interested in healthy eating
would feel bewildered on their first visit to a
health food shop : row upon row of unfamiliar
ingredients, from black-eye beans to wheatgerm.
This A–Z glossary gives details on
these foods and more, providing information on use,
preparation, cooking instructions and storage.
Health food cookery is simple and rewarding and
involves choosing the best ingredients available –
this section will arm you with a
comprehensive guide.*

Aduki bean

Very small, red beans with a sweet, nutty taste, aduki beans are the seed of a bushy plant which grows to about 25–75 cm (10–30 inches) in height.

Country of origin The aduki bean is native to Japan, but has been cultivated for centuries in China and Korea.

Uses In Japan and China the beans are usually left to ripen and are then used dried. They are soaked and boiled for use, usually as part of a main meal, or pounded into a fine paste and made into cakes. The beans are delicious added to soups, stews and salads as well as in rice dishes.

Cooking instructions Soak (see page 18), then cook for about 1 hour.

Storage They will keep for several years if stored in a tightly sealed container. Cooked beans will keep in the refrigerator for up to four days.

Aduki beans

14

Agar agar See *Kelp* (page 39).

Alfalfa

Known as lucerne or buffalo herb, alfalfa is one of the oldest cultivated herbs or plants. It is a deep-rooted plant which contains up to 19% protein, compared to beef which has 16% and milk with 3%. It is rich in calcium, iron, potassium, chlorine, sodium and magnesium, as well as being a good source of the necessary vitamins. It is one of the rare sources of vitamins B_{12}, K and U.

Country of origin Alfalfa was first grown by the Arabs for their horses, which developed remarkable strength.

Uses Used as a food supplement, especially in the Third World. Forms in which alfalfa is available are:—

Alfalfa powder A fairly strong tasting powder which can be added to soups and stews.

Alfalfa cereal Combined with other ingredients, it makes highly nutritious cereal.

Alfalfa flour Can be added in small quantities to other flours and used in any normal recipe.

Alfalfa tea The leaves of this plant are very rich in manganese and make a very beneficial tea.

Alfalfa sprouts See *Sprouting seeds* (page 59).

Almonds

These are the kernels of the fruit of the almond tree, of which there are sweet and bitter varieties.

Country of origin The almond tree itself is a native of the Eastern Mediterranean, but today almonds are widely grown in Jordan, Spain, North Africa, France and the United States.

Uses Sweet almonds, blanched, roasted, salted, sugared or ground, are used in making cakes, biscuits, desserts and savoury dishes and make an interesting, crunchy addition to salads, soups, fish or meat dishes.

Bitter almonds are rarely eaten, since they contain a small amount of poisonous prussic acid. When this is removed, the extracted almond oil can be used as a flavouring agent.

Cooking instructions Almonds may be blanched, roasted, ground or salted for use in cooking (see page 45).

Almond

Storage Store in an air-tight container in a cool place.

Apple cider vinegar

Vinegar was invented when the Stone Age man let his beer go sour and started to use the sour liquid for preserving many things, from food to hides. Apple cider vinegar is, however, considered very superior to all other vinegars, and is used in naturopathic medicine to heal a variety of illnesses and complaints.

Apple cider vinegar is very rich in potassium, phosphorus and calcium, with small amounts of iron, chlorine, sodium, magnesium, sulphur, fluoride, silicon and other trace elements.

Cider vinegar is available in a great variety of colours from light yellow to dark amber. This is due mainly to the differences in production, and some manufacturers add a small amount of burnt sugar caramel to make a rich brown colour. However, always buy cider vinegar which states quite clearly that it is made from the whole apple. Apple cider vinegar with honey is also marketed under the trade name of *honeygar*, which is quite easy to make yourself, using equal amounts of apple cider vinegar and honey.

Uses Use as a drink, gargle, flavouring for salad dressings and preservative. The general rule is to take two teaspoons of cider vinegar in a full glass of water and mix in a little honey. This is best taken first thing in the morning or drunk with any meal.

For a gargle when one has a sore throat, put one teaspoon in a glass of water and gargle with two mouthfuls of the solution every hour. Swallow the liquid after gargling.

Half a cup of cider vinegar added to the bath water is also said to bring relief to sufferers of skin disorders. Stay in the bath for at least 15 minutes. Rub dry with both hands, not with a towel.

Storage Store in a cool, dry place, making sure it is out of direct sunlight.

Barley

Barley may well be the oldest cultivated grain and was once probably the most important staple food in the world. Today, in the Western world it has largely been replaced by wheat.

Barley is a small, white grain with a fine, brownish line running down the centre, separating each grain into two tiny chambers. In the U.S.A. and Western Europe the grain is mainly eaten as pot barley or pearl barley. Pot barley is the whole grain minus the outer husk. It tastes nuttier than pearl barley, which lacks most of the bran and germ, as well as the husk.

Country of origin It is grown in India, Japan, the U.S.A and Western Europe.

Uses Barley is used in baby foods because it is easily digested. It can be made into a light, chewy breakfast cereal or added to soups and stews. Barley flour is fine and sweet and is especially good in biscuits and bread doughs.

Cooking instructions Cook in boiling water, as for rice, for about 45 minutes to make pilaf type dishes. To make barley porridge, dry roast 1 cup of barley in a pan over a high flame, until lightly browned. Place in a saucepan with 5 cups of water, bring to the boil and simmer for $1\frac{1}{2}$ hours. Add salt before serving.

Storage Barley will keep for about two months in a cool dry place.

Barley

Beans

High in food value and fine in flavour, dried peas and beans come as near the perfect vegetable as possible. Eaten fresh or dried, they provide a good and inexpensive source of protein. Beans have roughly double the protein of cereals, and more than meat, fish or eggs.

For millions of men, women and especially children, beans means baked beans in tomato sauce. Sad really, when there are as many as twenty different dried beans and peas with which to ring the changes. Ranging from the familiar haricot to the more exotic aduki, rose cocoa, black-eye and mung, there's a beanfeast of ideas for incorporating them into the daily diet.

There is every reason for making them a regular habit too, for dried peas and beans are bursting with protein. The master of the bean family, as far as food value is concerned, is the soya bean, which contains substantially more protein than meat, eggs or cheese. Most other beans share a similar food value. They are also low in available carbohydrate and fat so are a useful food for slimmers; cooked beans have a calorific value of 26 per ounce.

All beans are rich in iron, potassium and the B group vitamins, riboflavin and niacin, and, when sprouted, have the added bonus of vitamin C. Beans are also the richest source of vegetable fibre, providing roughage essential to the digestive system.

Not only can you use them in hearty soups, but they are a filling ingredient in casseroles, pot-roasts and other main meal dishes, and a substantial vegetable with cold meats and fish. Try them as a satisfying salad ingredient too.

Most peas and beans benefit from soaking before cooking – follow the easy guide below for perfect results, time and time again. Remember, however, that cooking time will lengthen with age as the beans become extra hard.

Storage Beans will keep for up to four days in the refrigerator when cooked. Store dry beans in sealed containers; they will keep indefinitely in a dry place.

Soaking instructions It is not essential to soak beans, but it shortens the cooking time, helps some varieties to hold their shape and helps to remove some of the oglio-saccharides which cause flatulence. Some cooks prefer to drain beans after soaking and cook in fresh, salted water; others feel that the soak water should not be discarded, since it contains vitamins and minerals. Choose the method you prefer.

For a quick soak, add 1·5–1·75 litres ($2\frac{3}{4}$–3 pints) hot water to 450 g (1 lb) beans. Bring to the boil and cook for 2 minutes. Cover and set aside for 1 hour before cooking.

For a regular soak, add 1·5 litres ($2\frac{3}{4}$ pints) cold water to 450 g (1 lb) beans. Leave to stand overnight, or for several hours, in a cool place before cooking. (Do not leave to soak for too long, or the beans may start to germinate).

Cooking instructions Drain the soaked beans and add 1·5 litres ($2\frac{3}{4}$ pints) fresh water, or leave in the soak water if preferred. Add 2 teaspoons salt and 1 tablespoon oil and cook until tender (see the individual guide for cooking times).

There are several types of bean to be found in health food shops, which are of a more exotic nature and are sometimes expensive. They are, however, worth sampling for their distinctive flavours:–

Flageolet These are pale green in colour and long and thin in shape. They are very good puréed, as for pease

Flageolet beans

18

Minted tomato ratatouille (see page 96); Creamy avocado pâté (see page 75)

pudding, and served with lamb. Cook the beans for about 1 hour.

Foule medame bean This bean has an unusually thick skin, with a dull brown appearance and slightly earthy taste and is about the size of a pea. It produces a thick meaty broth after long cooking – about 12 hours. Ordinary cooking takes about 1 hour.

Foule medame beans

Rose cocoa bean This is a longish, pink bean with darker flecks, with a noticeably sweet taste. Very good when cooked with lamb or apple for a pie. Cooking takes about 1 hour.

Rose cocoa beans

Black beans These are grown throughout India, Asia, Africa, China and the U.S.A. and are used mainly to produce bean sprouts. They are also cooked whole for soups, stews and savoury dishes. Cook for $1\frac{1}{2}$–2 hours.

Black beans

Split peas These are available, either as split peas with their skins taken away, or as whole dried peas with their skins still on. Cook for about 1–2 hours and use in meat-type loaves, patties, pies, stews etc.

Bean Sprouts See *Sprouting seeds* (page 59).

Split peas

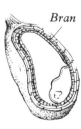

Bran

Bran is the tough, outer coating of the wheat grain, which is removed, together with the germ, during milling to produce white flour. It is a rich source of high quality protein, B vitamins and phosphorus.

It is composed mainly of fibre or roughage, which provides bulk in the intestines and is needed for the digestive system to function properly and efficiently. The lack of fibre in the everyday diet of Western man is linked with the growing incidence of degenerative diseases.

Recent research in the U.K. has proved that unprocessed, natural bran is better than refined bran cereal, although the latter is undoubtedly more appealing to those with little time to prepare their own breakfast cereals, using natural bran.

Uses Bran is delicious when added to other cereal grains and eaten with milk and honey, or added to other ingredients for baking savoury and fruit loaves, cakes and biscuits. Also gives an extra crispness and nuttiness to pastry.

Bran

Storage Keep in an air-tight container in a dry place.

Mixed bean salad (see page 99); Yogurt dressing (see page 111); Bean sprout salad (see page 98); Cracked wheat salad (see page 97)

Brazil nut

Also known as the para or cream nut, the Brazil nut, with its tough, angular shell, is the fruit of a large tree, grown originally in Brazil. Its taste is similar to that of the coconut and hazelnut.

Country of origin These nuts were first grown in Africa and South America.

Uses More often eaten plain as a dessert nut, they can be used in cooking and baking when sliced, chopped or ground.

Cooking instructions Brazil nuts may be blanched, roasted or ground for use in cooking.

Storage Store in an air-tight container in a cool place to prevent the nuts becoming soft or oily.

Black bean See *Beans* (page 17).

Black-eye bean

Brazil nut

A white, rounded bean, distinguished by a black mark like an eye at one side.

Country of origin The black-eye bean came originally from Africa, where it is still an important staple food, but it is now grown widely in America and in all tropical countries of the world, as well as Southern Europe.

Uses Dried, they are used in casseroles, rice dishes, soups and salads. In Africa, the dried seeds are ground into a coffee substitute. The young developing shoots are eaten like spinach and the tender pod is used as a green vegetable.

Cooking instructions Soak (see page 18) and cook for 1 hour.

Storage Dried black-eye beans will keep for several years in a tightly sealed container. Cooked beans will keep for four days in the refrigerator.

Brewers' yeast

Brewers' yeast is a by-product of the brewing process, and has outstanding nutritional qualities. Brewers' yeast contains 16 of the 20 amino acids and the whole range of B complex vitamins. It is particularly rich in vitamins B_1 and B_2. It also contains large amounts of phosphorus, iron and calcium.

Black-eye beans

B vitamins are perhaps the easiest of all vitamins in which to become deficient. This is because they can easily be destroyed by cooking, and many of them cannot be stored. Symptoms of deficiency include depression, fatigue, skin irritations, sores of the mouth and palpitations, the most serious diseases being beri-beri and pellagra.

Uses There are many types of brewers' yeast, with varying taste and composition. Brewers' yeast is available in tablet form, but perhaps the easiest way to put it on the menu is in the form of dried powder. It is very digestible in a 'pep-up' drink with orange juice. Add it to soups, gravies and casseroles too.

Instructions for use It is wise to start taking brewers' yeast gradually, beginning with ½ teaspoon and then increasing to 1 teaspoon daily.

Storage Keep in an air-tight container in a cool, dry place.

Broad bean

A very large, flat, brown bean, it is also known as the Windsor bean, haba or horse bean.

Country of origin Broad beans can be traced back to the Swiss lake dwellings of the Bronze Age, but found popularity with the Egyptians, Greeks and Romans as a staple food for the masses. It is grown extensively in France and South America.

Uses They are especially good in dark, meaty casseroles, but in Brazil they are roasted and pounded into a flour. Many poor South Americans make up huge pots of broad beans, which are reheated day after day, and these are known as 'awakened beans'.

Cooking instructions Dried broad beans need to be soaked (see page 18), then cooked for about 1½ hours.

Storage Dried broad beans will keep for several years stored in an air-tight container.

Brown rice See *Rice* (page 52).

Bulgur

Bulgur is a wheat product, which has survived from ancient times in Eastern Europe. It is usually sold as cooked, parboiled wheat. Bulgur has an excellent

Broad beans

23

nutritional value with almost 12% protein and is a good source of phosphorus, iron and B vitamins.

There are basically two types of bulgur:–

Parboiled (parched) bulgur Most manufacturers will parboil the grain before pearling. This bulgur will be sold as precooked on the label, and therefore has a shorter cooking time.

Bulgur flour This flour is heavy in consistency and needs refrigerating, since it contains the germ of the grain. It is not widely available in shops.

Uses Use as one would wheat in bread, cakes, biscuits and pastry making. As a grain, it can be cooked like rice and used in rice-type dishes such as paella, risotto and pilaf.

Cooking instructions Use one cup of grain bulgur to two cups of water. Bring to the boil and simmer gently for about 15–20 minutes.

Storage Store in a cool, dry place. Bulgur flour must be refrigerated and keeps for only about one week.

Bulgur

Buckwheat

Also called Saracen corn, it is not a grain as such, since it is related to the dock and rhubarb in the botanical sense. The plant has attractive, heart-shaped leaves and pale pink flowers.

It is relatively rich in protein, rich in iron and contains almost the entire range of B complex vitamins. The ructic acid content of buckwheat places it high on the list of curative plants. Ructic acid has a powerful effect on the arteries and circulatory system.

Buckwheat is available in many forms:–

Rutin tablets These are available from health food stores and are to be taken internally.

Buckwheat flour This tends to be more expensive than other flours because of the difficulty in removing the sheathlike husk. The flour can be used in muffins, pancakes and biscuit recipes. It is most successful in recipes which call for a heavier flour. Many recipes advise mixing buckwheat with other flours such as rice or wheat, to lighten it.

Buckwheat groats These are the crushed and hulled seeds of the plant. They look very much like the

Buckwheat

beechnut. The groats may be cooked like rice, simmering gently in water until soft, or they may be used for their crunchy texture in biscuits or a type of buckwheat brittle.

Kasha This is the name given to roasted buckwheat.

Uses Buckwheat is widely used as a food and accompaniment for game, for buckwheat cakes and even for brewing beer and other drinks in Germany. Buckwheat honey is also very popular in Russia.

Storage Flour, rice and groats should be stored in an air-tight container in a cool, dry place.

Butter bean See *Lima bean* (page 41).

Carageen moss See *Kelp* (page 39).

Cashew nut

These are the kidney-shaped seeds of a tropical tree called *Anacardium Occidentale*.

Country of origin Formerly native to Brazil, cashews are now grown throughout South America and India.

Uses Most imported cashew nuts have already been roasted and had their outer layer removed, since it contains an acrid fluid which produces blisters on contact with the skin.

Ground, chopped, roasted or salted, cashew nuts are used as an ingredient in cakes, salads, desserts, nut roasts and as a cocktail snack.

Cooking instructions Cashews may be blanched, roasted, ground or salted for use in cooking (see page 45).

Storage Store in an air-tight container in a cool place.

Cashew nut

Chestnut

The chestnut is the large brown nut of the *Castenea* tree, the best known varieties being the sweet or Spanish chestnut and the Japanese chestnut.

Country of origin The sweet chestnut tree is native to the Mediterranean, where hundreds of different varieties

25

Chestnut

grow wild. Today, they are grown in North America, France and Southern Europe. Chestnuts grown in Britain are small and hard to peel, therefore most of the chestnuts sold in shops are imported from either France or Italy. They are in season during the winter months.

Uses Sweet and floury when cooked, chestnuts are used boiled, puréed, roasted and chopped in soups and sauces, for stuffings and garnishings and as a sweet ingredient in cake fillings, puddings and ices. When steeped and cooked in syrup they are called marrons glacés.

Cooking instructions The simplest way to peel chestnuts is to make a slit in the hard skin at the pointed end of the nut with a sharp knife, and place them in an ovenproof dish with a little water. Bake in a hot oven (220°C, 425°F, Gas Mark 7) for 8 minutes. Leave to cool, then peel.

To cook, place the peeled chestnuts in a saucepan of boiling water and simmer gently over a low heat for 45–60 minutes, or until they are tender.

To roast chestnuts, slit the pointed ends and roast in front of an open fire, under a hot grill or in a moderately hot oven (200°C, 400°F, Gas Mark 6) for about 20 minutes, or until the shells split open and the chestnuts are golden brown.

Storage Chestnuts do not keep well at room temperature. They will keep for a few months in the refrigerator if stored in a ventilated container. Whole, shelled chestnuts can be blanched and frozen.

Chick pea

The chick pea, also known as the garbanzo pea, Bengal gram or Egyptian pea can be white, yellow, brown, even red or black, but the most popular is corn-coloured, about the size of a hazelnut with an earthy flavour.

Country of origin Wild chick peas grew in Egypt in the time of the Pharoahs, although it is thought that they originated in Western Asia. Today they are commercially grown in America, Africa and Australia.

Uses They are eaten widely in South-west France, Spain, Turkey and India as well as Africa, where they are used for the classic couscous. Chick peas are also of major importance in almost all Mediterranean countries, where they are ground into a paste and mixed with garlic, oil and lemon juice to make hummus. They can also be boiled, baked or ground into a flour.

Chick pea

Cooking instructions Dried chick peas should be soaked (see page 18) then cooked for about 45 minutes.

Storage Dried chick peas will keep for several years if stored in an air-tight container in a cool place.

Cob nuts See *Hazelnuts* (page 35).

Coconut

Coconuts are the fruit of the coconut palm. The coconut consists of an outer fibrous husk containing the white flesh and coconut milk.

Country of origin The coconut palm originated in Malaya but now grows freely in all the tropical regions of the world.

Uses Coconut milk is often used as a substitute for water or cows milk when preparing puddings and desserts.

Coconut

The flesh is often eaten fresh or is cooked to extract its oil. It is used to make coconut butter and coconut cream, for flavouring and garnishing, and in salads, desserts and sauces.

The dried kernel is grated to produce desiccated coconut, which is used with rice, in curries and made into sweetmeats. Commercially known as copra, it is used to make margarines, soap, cosmetics and coconut oil.

Cooking instructions The kernel is drained of its milk by spiking the soft eyes in the top of the husk. The kernel may then be split with a heavy blade or hammer and the white coconut flesh can be removed.

Storage Store desiccated coconut in a sealed container in a cool place. Fresh coconut in water will keep fresh in the refrigerator for several days if the water is changed daily.

Coffee

Coffee contains caffeine, a powerful stimulant belonging to the alkaloids family. Caffeine can raise the basal metabolic rate of the body by up to 10% and cause anxiety, insomnia and high blood pressure. It is for this reason that many coffee substitutes, which have positive health benefits have found their way on to the market.

Dandelion coffee This is one of the most delicious coffee substitutes. It is usually bought as an instant powder, but you can make it yourself. Simply dig up the

roots of dandelion plants in the autumn, snip off the crowns, wash the roots gently, and dry with kitchen paper. Bake in a cool oven until quite dry; turn up the heat when they are nearly dry to crisp the outsides. Store in an air-tight tin and grind just before use.

Grain coffees These are coffees based on toasted grains. One contains rye, oats, millet, barley, figs and chicory, another, equally popular, is made from toasted bran, wheat and molasses. These grains need gentle boiling to bring out the flavour and actually improve with reheating.

Postum This is the traditional coffee substitute and cannot be made at home. It is manufactured by mixing molasses and bran and roasting them at a high temperature. Red wheat is then added, and the ingredients are finely ground. Add boiling water.

Swiss coffee substitutes These drinks contain fruit and roots as well as grains and cereals.

Decaffeinated coffee It has generally been thought that, if a regular intake of caffeine is to be avoided, it might reasonably be supposed that decaffeinated coffee would be an acceptable substitute. Unfortunately, American tests have now revealed that the chemical used to remove the caffeine often remains in the coffee and it too is undesirable.

Dandelion roots

Common bean

Varieties of common bean are the French bean, haricot bean, navy bean, pinto bean, snap bean and kidney bean. Haricot is the bean commonly used in 'baked beans in tomato sauce' and, as such, is the most popular bean in the world.

Country of origin Kidney beans have been cultivated in North America since prehistoric times, and were brought to Europe in the sixteenth century. They reached England from France in 1594 and were referred to as French beans.

Red kidney beans

Red kidney bean Plump, red and shiny, the beans are used in the classic chilli con carne, and are particularly good in salads too.

Haricot or navy beans These small, roundish white beans are used in soups, stews and savoury dishes and in the classic slow-cooked cassoulet, the bean and pork dish from France.

Haricot beans

28

Cannellini beans These are long, white beans which contrast well when mixed with haricot beans.

Cooking instructions Dried common beans should be soaked (see page 18), then cooked for about 1 hour.

Storage Dried beans will keep for several years if kept in a cool place in an air-tight container.

Cannellini beans

Corn (maize)

There are many distinctly different varieties of corn existing today, most of them highly developed hybrids, quite different from the tiny husks of wild corn found by the natives of South America thousands of years ago.

There are seven main types of corn, available in one form or another:–

Sweet corn Often called corn on the cob, it is the vegetable version of the maize plant. It is intended to be eaten as a vegetable, since it is far too sweet to be dried and ground into a flour.

Flint corn This is a very long, thin corn which has a hard endosperm. It is therefore difficult to grind and is now mainly fed to animals.

Dent corn This is the corn most widely available commercially in the U.S.A. When the hard endosperm dries it 'dents' the top of the corn. Corn meal and flour are ground from this grain.

Flour corn This is the top quality field corn. Flour corn has a very thin endosperm and soft starchy kernels.

Popcorn Unfortunately the poorest, nutritionally, of all the maize grains, but it is used extensively by sweet manufacturers.

Corn flour This is generally made from the hard and soft starch layers, which lie directly under the hard seed casing. It does not include the germ, which contains all the nutrients. Corn flour is often processed to make it very white. It is a good thickening agent, but adds little nutritional value to the food.

Corn meal Always buy stoneground whole corn meal when corn meal is stated in a recipe. This is because the grain has sometimes been degerminated, which literally means that the germ has been taken out. Sifted or bolted corn meal simply means that the hulled, ground grain has been put through a mesh to get a finer texture.

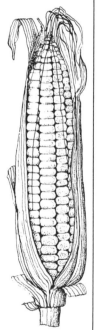

Corn on the cob

29

Country of origin The main exporter of corn is the U.S.A.

Uses As a flour it is used for thickening, as a cornmeal for puddings and cakes, breads and cereal. Fresh corn is delicious as a vegetable and with rice mixtures. The dry grain is not suitable for cooking the way we would prepare other grains such as wheat or barley.

Cooking instructions Cook corn on the cob for about 8–10 minutes and corn kernels for about 6–8 minutes.

Storage Store in a cool, dry place. In the case of cornflour, use an air-tight container.

Corn oil

Corn oil, as the name suggests, is oil compressed from the grain corn. It is high in linoleic acid, about 40%, which makes it 60% saturated. It also contains amounts of oleic, linolenic and arachidic acids. It is a rich source of phosphorus and the fat soluble vitamins A, D and E.

Country of origin Corn has been pressed for its oils ever since the Peruvians began cultivation thousands of years ago. Today our major source of corn oil is the U.S.A.

Uses Corn oil is a popular addition to margarine and other foods. As a cooking medium, it is light and easily digested. The oil has also been found to correct over-alkalinity of the body and restore it to its correct balance. Doctors also recommend it in cases of bad eczema and skin disorders, for which it is either taken internally or applied to the skin.

Storage Corn oil keeps well in a cool, dark place.

Cracked wheat See *Wheat* (page 63).

Currants

These are the dried fruit of the tiny, purple Corinth grape. Smallest of all the dried fruits, it has a hard, crisp texture, a tarter flavour than raisins or sultanas, and is fairly rich in minerals.

Country of origin Currants came originally from Greece, which is still the major exporter.

Currants

Uses Use in sauces, cakes, desserts, biscuits, pastries and salads.

Cooking instructions Wash carefully in hot water and

dry before use, unless guaranteed unsprayed with mineral oil.

Storage Stored in an air-tight container, currants will keep well for up to one year. Currants also freeze well.

Dates

The date, along with the fig, is one of the oldest known cultivated fruits. It has been in cultivation for more than seven thousand years and it is the universal provider of the Arab world. The fruit crop from one tree is enormous, more than 45 kg (100 lb) a year, and a tree may live for a century. When fresh and ripe it is amber in colour but is darker brown when dried.

Country of origin The date was first grown in the fertile crescent between the Tigris and Euphrates, seven thousand years ago. The world's most popular date, the Deglet Noor, is the one which was introduced into California in the early years of the twentieth century and is now the variety grown most in the U.S.A. Dates are also grown in Iraq and North Africa.

Uses The fruit is delicious eaten ripe from the palm, but many dates keep well when dried. Sugar and wine are made from the tree's sap, oil is extracted from the seeds and rope is made from its fibres. Dates, both fresh and dried, are used mainly in making cakes, biscuits, pastries and puddings, but may also be eaten raw as a sweetmeat, in salads and in fruit cups. As a garnish or decoration, dates can be stuffed with cream cheese, almonds or candied fruit. The best dates are packed whole in long boxes. Poorer quality dates are stoned, compressed and sold by weight for use in baking.

Cooking instructions Carefully peel the skin from fresh dates before use.

Storage Stored in an air-tight container, dates will keep for up to six months.

Dates

Dried apricots

The dried flesh of the golden stone fruit, apricots contain more protein than any other dried fruit and are a good source of Vitamin C.

Country of origin Although apricot trees were first cultivated in China, apricot stones were taken by traders to Europe via the Middle East, and finally to California, where the first methods of drying fruits were developed. Most of our dried apricots today come from Australia, Iran, Turkey and California.

Uses Use chopped in sauces, stuffings, cakes and desserts and whole in fruit salads, meat dishes and rich puddings.

Cooking instructions If dried apricots need to be soaked before use in cooking, soak in cold water for at least 6 hours or overnight.

Storage Stored in an air-tight container, dried apricots will keep well for up to one year. Dried apricots also freeze well.

Dried fruit

Dried fruit

Dried fruit is a valuable source of nourishment for the health food enthusiast, since it contains the goodness of fresh fruit in a concentrated form.

Most fruit is dried by warmth, much of it in the natural heat of the sun, but today, more and more is dried by artificial heat. It is now possible, however, to dry fruit by freezing it at very low temperatures. It is then transferred to a vacuum chamber, where the ice crystals turn into vapour without first becoming liquid. The finished product is not frozen but dried, with a moisture content as low as 2%.

The most ancient, and still the most popular, dried fruits are dates, prunes, figs and grapes (as raisins, currants and sultanas), although dried apricots, peaches, bananas, apples and pears are increasing in availability.

Dried fruits are a rich source of protein, vitamins and minerals. Dates are rich in niacin and also contain some carotene, thiamine and riboflavin. Figs, as well as being rich in a whole range of minerals, have an especially high iron content. Sultanas, raisins and currants are rich in iron and potassium as well as in the invert sugar, fructose. Dried peaches contain an astonishing amount of iron and dried apples retain all their vitamin C.

As well as selling the fruits individually, most health food stores also make up their own packs of dried fruit salad, containing dried apples, pears, prunes, bananas, apricots and peaches, as well as a wide selection of mixed dried fruits for cake making.

Feteritas See *Sorghum* (page 56).

Figs

The fig tree is less versatile than the date palm, and interest in it is confined to the fruit. Fresh figs are thin-skinned and suffer if they have to travel, but there are no problems when they have been dried. This is usually done in the sun and the sugar forms a deposit on the skin.

Country of origin Originally from Asia, figs are now grown in many hot climates.

Uses Figs are often available fresh and can always be bought dried. Eat raw as an hors d'oeuvre or stewed as a dessert, with cream and lemon juice or peeled in port wine, or with cheese.

Cooking instructions Peel carefully if required, or stew gently in a little water until tender – about 10–15 minutes.

Storage Dried figs will keep fresh in an air-tight container for up to one year.

Figs

Filberts See *Hazelnuts* (page 35).

Flageolet See *Beans* (page 17).

Flour See *Wheat* (page 63).

Foule medame bean See *Beans* (page 17).

Foxtail millet See *Millet* (page 42).

Garlic

Garlic, one of the most versatile natural flavouring agents, comes in many varieties, some having white skinned bulbs, the skin of others being pink or mauve. The bulbs vary greatly in size too, as do the number of cloves they contain – some cloves are very small, but there are giant forms. The flavour varies according to type and the climate in which it is grown. Some garlic is

Garlic

mild, sweet and almost nutty, while other types are exceedingly strong in flavour. The best garlic comes from the warmer climates – garlic grown in cold or damp areas is liable to be rank and ill-flavoured.

Good garlic is hard, the cloves are not shrunk away from the paperlike sheath and there are no discoloured spots.

Garlic is also thought of as being extremely health-giving. It contains antiseptic substances which tone up the digestive system, it reduces blood pressure and helps to clear bronchitis. In the past it was known as 'poor man's or churl's treacle – treacle originally meant an antidote for poisons, stings and bites. Roman soldiers used to eat garlic as a stimulant before going into battle and it was also given to cocks before a fight.

Country of origin Garlic is probably native to Asia, but has been cultivated near the Mediterranean since the days of the Ancient Egyptians. Today it is grown in warm countries all over the world.

Uses A whole clove of garlic can give piquancy to a sauce, stew or casserole, and a clove dropped into French dressing will add zest to any salad.

Cooking instructions Garlic is a concentrated flavouring and it improves a vast number of dishes. If very little flavouring is required, the standard method is to rub a cut clove over the dish, salad bowl or joint of meat. For a stronger flavour, put a peeled clove through a garlic press or chop it finely. A quick Spanish trick is to put the peeled clove under a flat kitchen knife and squash it with a sharp blow before chopping.

Storage Keep in a cool, dry place.

Ginseng

A strange, man-like root from the plant *Panax Ginseng*, it is valued very highly for its properties as a tonic and restorative. It is used in the treatment of diseases and to increase sexual activity.

The plants like to grow in deep, sandy soil away from stagnant water. At least five years are needed for the roots to develop properly, hence its very high price.

The medicinal properties of ginseng are attributed to substances found in the root. The active principles have been identified as six individual glycosides, called panaxosides. Ginseng also contains amino acids, organic acids, sterols, flavonoids and vitamins.

The Russians have shown that ginseng acts on the body to prevent the effects of stress, normalising the chemical changes it causes in the body.

Ginseng can be bought in root, powder, extract and tablet form.

Country of origin The ancient Chinese were the first to use ginseng, and have been doing so throughout the centuries to the present day. Ginseng grows wild in North America and Siberia but American ginseng is the most popular for commercial export. Ginseng is sold commercially in several main categories. The Chinese and Korean variety is the true ginseng, and is now cultivated in Japan. Wild Chinese ginseng is sometimes called Manchurian ginseng. Cultivated roots from both China and Korea are sometimes sold as Asiatic ginseng. These can be red or white, depending upon the curing.

Uses Ginseng has been used for centuries to prevent disease and as a general tonic. Russian tests have also shown that ginseng acts as a stimulant to the central nervous system, actually increasing the efficiency of cerebral activity. Brain patterns were shown to increase in speed. However it is said 'Ginseng, in contrast to other stimulants, causes no disturbance in the equilibrium of the cerebral processes. This explains the absence of any pronounced sense of subjective excitement as is characteristic of other stimulants . . . and also why this stimulant does not interfere with the normal bodily functions.' *Professor Petkov – Institute of Advanced Medical Training in Sofia.*

Ground nut oil See *Peanut oil* (page 49).

Ginseng

Hazelnuts (cob nuts and filberts)

These are closely related members of the *Corylus* family of trees. Hazelnuts and cob nuts are small and round, whereas filberts are larger, oval nuts.

Country of origin The nuts grow wild in Europe, North America, Asia and the Middle East.

Uses Hazelnuts are usually lightly baked before being used in cakes, confectionery, puddings and sorbets. Filberts are more generally used for dessert purposes.

Hazelnut

35

Cooking instructions Blanch, roast or grind for use as on previous page.

Storage Store in a sealed container in a cool, dry place.

Herbal teas

Herb teas offer the health food enthusiast an excellent opportunity to absorb the health-giving qualities of plants. There are many varieties, available either in dry leaf or tea bag form.

It is easy to buy a variety of herbs and mix them yourself. Stronger leaves should be balanced with milder flavours, or a blend can be made up to help a specific complaint.

Some of the complaints which can be treated with infused herbs are:–
Arthritis Comfrey, dandelion and buckwheat
Asthma Nettle, coltsfoot and marjoram
Bladder disorders Buchu, couch grass, dandelion and parsley
Bronchitis Anise, borage, cicely, coltsfoot, comfrey and elder
Catarrh Balm, cicely, coltsfoot, elder and thyme
Colds Elderflower, peppermint, tansy, thyme, sage, and coltsfoot
Cystitis Buchu, couch grass, and marshmallow
Digestive complaints Anise, basil, chamomile, cicely, dandelion, fennel, hyssop, mint, parsley, tansy and thyme
Fatigue Dandelion, nettle, angelica, dill and sage
Insomnia Chamomile, lime and cowslip
Rheumatism Comfrey, couch grass, cowslip and hyssop
Sprains Comfrey, buckwheat and marshmallow
Varicose veins Buckwheat and lime

Some of the complaints which can be treated with decocted herbs are:–
Arthritis and rheumatism Celery seeds
Eczema and skin complaints Dandelion roots
General vitality Sarsaparilla plant root
Slimming and gastric troubles Fenugreek seed

Preparation instructions There are two ways to prepare herbal teas:–

To infuse, pour boiling water on the leaves, in much the same way as you would make tea. Use only stainless steel or ceramic containers. Use one teaspoon of leaves for each cup of water. Allow to steep for 5–10 minutes, with the lid on the pot or with the container covered. Strain and flavour with a piece of lemon or a spoonful of honey.

For a decoction the herbs are gently boiled. Use about 2 teaspoons of seeds, roots, etc., for each 600 ml (1 pint) of water. Bring to the boil, cover and simmer for about 15 minutes. Pour into a teapot or jug, cover and steep for a few more minutes before pouring.

Hiziki See *Kelp* (page 39).

Honey

Honey has assumed an almost mystical quality over the centuries; the Prophet Mohammed said 'Honey is a remedy for every illness' and the ancient Egyptians dressed wounds and burns with honey and used it in many potent medicines.

Honey is produced from the flowers of plants and trees. This nectar first consists of a weak solution of sugars in water, and is carried to the hive in the honey stomach of the bee. Sucrose is converted into the predigested sugars levulose and dextrose by the enzymes present in the bee's stomach.

Bee collecting nectar

The bee deposits the nectar in the honeycombs of the hive, where the process of conversion continues. A large amount of water gradually evaporates in the warmth of the hive. The bees cap the honey with wax when it is ripe.

The actual composition of honey will depend upon the flowers, the weather, the season and other variations of nature.

Honey contains vitamins B_1, B_2, B_3, pantothenic acid, B_6, biotin and folic acid. It can contain large amounts of vitamin C. Naturally, this varies with the type of nectar.

The minerals in honey are important – iron, copper, sodium, potassium, manganese, calcium, magnesium, and phosphorus are present. The sugars play a major role, as do the acids. Honey also contains several enzymes. Generally speaking, the darker the honey, the more minerals and vitamins are present.

Honey is valuable for several reasons; since the bee has predigested the nectar, the honey can go straight into the bloodstream. This makes it a powerful boost to energy and it is therefore much appreciated by athletes.

Another outstanding property is its hygroscopicity, which means that it attracts moisture. This makes it a

37

great natural healer because disease germs need water to multiply. Honey is also a natural antiseptic and antibiotic.

Although honey has been used for about 15,000 years, and been subjected to close laboratory tests, there are several ingredients which still defy analysis. Doctor Jarvis, the authority on folk medicine in the U.S.A., gives several reasons for using honey and not sugar: honey is non-irritating to the lining of the digestive tract. It is easily and rapidly assimilated, and quickly furnishes the demand for energy, enabling athletes and others who expend energy heavily, to recuperate rapidly from exertion. It also has a natural and gentle laxative effect, and a sedative value. It is easier for the kidneys to process honey than any of the other sugars.

Honey can replace sugar in most recipes, but when doing so, use only three-quarters the amount of honey instead of sugar. Any liquid must be reduced by a fifth for each half cup of honey used.

Assorted honey products are available in health food shops :–

Propolis This is the substance used by bees to glue the hive together. The bees inject it with enzymes and antibiotics and many claims have been made for its medicinal value. It is available in liquid and tablet form, and also in pleasant tasting sweets.

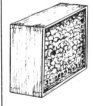

Honeycomb

Pollen tablets An extraction and elimination process has produced an extract of pollen without the factors to which many people are allergic. Some nations use this tablet for training athletes.

Honeycombs These are the hexagonal cells of wax, made by the bees to support the honey. Many people chew it to relieve hay-fever and sinus complaints.

Bee brood This is made of baby bees. In some places, bees do not survive the winter and the colony is killed off. The colony contains bee larvae and pupae, rich in vitamins A and D and protein. The larvae are marketed as a delicacy and can be fried, smoked or grilled.

Royal jelly This is a jelly-like honey which the bees make to feed the young queen. It is rich in enzymes and natural hormones. Royal jelly is widely used and is marketed in the form of health tablets, cosmetics and food. A worker bee can be turned into a queen simply by eating this substance.

Honey cappings When the honey is ripe, the bee caps it with a layer of wax. Research has shown that this has its own particular health-giving properties, somewhat similar to honeycomb.

Mead Diluted honey is fermented to make this alcoholic drink, which was the traditional English banqueting drink until the Middle Ages, when it was superseded by wine. The mallic acid in mead is alleged to counteract gout and rheumatism.

To obtain some cheaper brands of honey, the bees are fed on a sugar solution placed just outside the hive. This means that the complicated enzyme reaction and the minerals are missing.

Storage Honey should always be kept covered, in a dry place at room temperature. Tight-fitting lids are best. Honey tends to go darker and taste stronger with age. It may crystallise with very old age, or if the temperature is too cool. To make it liquid again, place the honey pot in a pan of warm water.

Honeygar See *Apple cider vinegar* (page 16).

9

Iodised salt See *Salt* (page 55).

J

Jumbo oats See *Oatmeal* (page 45).

K

Kafir See *Sorghum* (page 56).

Kasha See *Buckwheat* (page 24).

Kelp

Seaweed is possibly the oldest sea crop known to man. The Romans, Greeks and Chinese used it as a food, medicine and fertiliser.

Kelp

Kelp is a member of the seaweed family. It grows deep in the rocky bottoms of the ocean, taking hold on the rocks with tentacles. There are nearly one thousand varieties of kelp. The most popular one, used in the preparation of kelp tablets and granules, is called *Macrocystis Pyrifera*. Other members of the group include laver, agar agar, carageen, Irish moss and Icelandic moss.

Kelp contains 13 vitamins, 20 essential amino acids and 60 trace elements. It is also an excellent source of iodine, and vitamins A, B_1, B_2, B_{12}, C and D.

Uses Kelp is available in several forms, but mainly as a powder or tablet. The powder may be added in very small quantities to stews and casseroles, but a good way to include kelp in the diet is in the form of the products below:–

Agar agar This has strong jelling properties and is widely available as a powder. It may be used instead of commercial gelatine.

Hiziki This is seaweed, packaged in long, thin strands. This may be boiled and used in much the same way as pasta or spaghetti.

Kombu This is seaweed, sold in thick green strands or cut more finely, like hiziki.

Wakame Sold in sprouts or bunches, wakame must be carefully picked over for tough stems.

Nori Similar to wakame, nori is sold in thin sheets.

Carageen moss and dulse These are available dried and packaged, and should be simmered slowly until similar in consistency to jelly. Add honey, yogurt, fruit and fruit juices for a pleasing dish.

Laver or sea lettuce This looks like spinach and may be gathered around the coast at low tide. Laver is widely available in Wales, where it is fried and served with eggs and bacon.

Storage Dried kelp stores well for up to one year in a cool, dry place.

Kibbled wheat See *Wheat* (page 63).

Kidney bean See *Common bean* (page 28).

Kombu See *Kelp* (page 39).

𝓛

Lentils

Lentils are leguminous seeds, about half the size of a pea, the most usual being the orange or Egyptian lentil. Other varieties include the green or greenish brown lentil which is larger. Lentils are richer in protein than any other pulse with the exception of the soya bean. There are two main types of lentil, the Chinese and the Indian. The Chinese lentils vary from white to green and the Indian are various shades of pink and red.

Country of origin Lentils were one of the first cultivated crops in the East. They were introduced to the U.S.A. in 1914 and have since become an important crop to the country.

Uses Lentils are used in making casseroles and stews, vegetable-type rissoles and patties as well as thick, rich soups.

Cooking instructions Since lentils cook quite quickly, it is not necessary to soak them. However, some experts think that soaking makes them more digestible. Cooking time after soaking is about 1 hour.

Storage In a cool, dry place, lentils will keep almost indefinitely.

Lentils

Lima bean

These are also known as the butter bean, sieva bean, curry bean or pole bean.

Country of origin As the name suggests, lima beans come from Lima in Peru. But long before Columbus made his voyage of discovery, the bean was growing throughout America. Today it is grown in all tropical areas of the world. The species produces two distinct groups, the large, flat butter bean – a favourite in British cooking, and the smaller sieva bean.

Uses Available canned, dried or frozen, butter beans are often served as a vegetable with traditional boiled bacon or Sunday roast.

Cooking instructions After soaking dried lima beans (see page 18), cook for about 1½ hours or until tender.

Storage Dried lima beans will keep for several years if they are stored in an air-tight container in a cool place.

Lima beans

41

𝓜

Maize See *Corn* (page 29).

Millet

Millet

Millet was possibly the first cereal grain to be used for domestic purposes, and was a staple food in China before rice was introduced about 12,000 years ago. It is still an important staple food in parts of Africa such as Ethiopia, and in India and Asia.

All whole grain millet has been hulled, since the outer casing is so hard that not even budgerigars can crack it. The most common types of millet generally available are:–

Foxtail millet also known as Italian or yellow millet.

Pearl millet also known as bulrush, cat tail or candle millet.

Prosso also known as broomcorn or hog millet.

Foxtail millet

Country of origin Millet was first grown in Africa, India, Asia and China.

Millet flour since millet is such a small grain, the flour is only marginally more nutritious on a weight for weight basis than the whole grain. It is used primarily as a tasty and nutritious thickening agent and to add colour and flavour to soups and casseroles.

Millet lacks gluten, so bread made with millet flour will not rise very well. The national loaf of Ethiopia, injera, is made from millet flour.

Uses Serve as a grain, similar to rice, for vegetable and grain mixtures, in stews, with eggs for a soufflé and all savoury-type dishes.

Cooking instructions When cooked, this grain should be white and fluffy. After rinsing, dry-roast in a pan to remove the water. Sauté in a little oil to bring out the flavour of the grain, then bring to the boil and simmer until tender – about 30 minutes.

Storage Store in a cool, dry place.

Milo See *Sorghum* (page 56).

Mineral waters See *Water* (page 63).

Miso See *Soya bean* (page 57).

Molasses

Molasses, also known as blackstrap molasses, is a by-product of the sugar refining industry. The sugar cane is crushed and processed to obtain refined, white sugar and the residue, after this process has been completed, is called molasses.

Thick dark molasses is a rich source of nutrients. Generally speaking, the darker the colour, the richer the nutritive value. The darkest molasses is blackstrap.

Dark molasses is a good source of many of the B vitamins, especially inositol and B6. It is rich in iron, copper, calcium, phosphorus and potassium. It contains more iron, on a weight for weight basis, than liver, and several times more than milk.

Uses Available in tins and jars, it can be diluted with a little warm water and stirred into milk shakes. It can also be substituted for honey in all cake, fruit and bread recipes see *Honey* (page 37). Many meat dishes are delicious with molasses.

Storage Store in a cool, dry place with the lid firmly sealed for up to six months.

Molasses

Muesli

Muesli was first formulated by Doctor Bircher-Benner in Zurich, about 70 years ago. In Britain, America and Australia it has come to be regarded as a breakfast cereal, based on rolled oats with fresh or dried fruit, served with milk or yogurt.

The muesli marketed today, as based on the original Bircher-Benner formula, contains ten ingredients; wheat, oats, millet, unrefined sugar, dried apples, sultanas, roasted hazelnuts, roasted almonds, wheat germ and dried skimmed milk.

Nutritionally, this provides a complete protein, a rich source of calcium and the vitamin B complex group, plus a good range of the vitamins, A, D, C and E.

It is much cheaper to make your own muesli than to buy packets; experiment and find the flavours and textures your family likes best (see recipes on page 70).

Storage Muesli can be stored in a screw-topped jar for several months.

43

Mung bean

Also known as the green gram, golden gram, black gram or Oregon pea, it is the most popular of the sprouting beans (see *Sprouting seeds* page 59). The mung species have several main varieties, ranging in colour from green through yellow and golden to black. The green-seeded types are generally used for cooking or sprouting.

Country of Origin First cultivated in India, the mung bean quickly became widespread and popular throughout Asia.

Uses When sprouted they are used in salads and stir-fried dishes with fish, meat and poultry. Whole, dried mung beans are eaten in stews, casseroles and savoury dishes, or in the East as a porridge.

Cooking instructions Whole, dried beans should be soaked (see page 18), then cooked for 1 hour. Sprouted beans should be cooked very quickly for 1–2 minutes.

Storage Dried mung beans will keep for several years in an air-tight container in a cool place. Store sprouted beans in the refrigerator for one to two days.

Mung beans

Nori See *Kelp* (page 39).

Nuts

Nuts are probably the most valuable food to the vegetarian or health food enthusiast, since they are high in proteins and fats, and rich in B vitamins and minerals. They provide texture and a savoury quality in salads, cooked vegetables, grains and dried fruit, as well as being a delicious food in their own right.

Almonds, hazelnuts, cashews and peanuts are particularly flavourful when roasted and added to sauces, cooked rice or wheat grain, or sprinkled on a salad. Add to muesli, baked fruit and nut bars, or use as a topping for breads and cakes.

Walnuts, Brazil nuts, cashews and hazelnuts, finely ground, raw or roasted, are a good basis for nut roasts, savoury dishes and cocktail savouries.

Before use in cooking, nuts often have to be blanched, roasted or ground. Follow the easy guide below for perfect results, time and time again. To ring the changes, try salting your own nuts for quick snacks and tasty nibbles.

Nuts tend to be expensive items on the shopping list, and are therefore often relegated to the luxury food category, but, weight for weight, they provide excellent nutritional value and form the basis for many a tasty meal. With a little imagination, nuts can appear more often than at Christmas feasts and in the occasional cake mixture.

Blanching Place the nuts in a small bowl and cover with boiling water. Leave for about 3 minutes. Remove, one at a time with a spoon, and press between the thumb and the forefinger. The skin should slip off easily. Dry the nuts on a cloth.

Blanching

If the nuts are not to be used immediately, put them on a rack in a very cool oven (110°C, 225°F, Gas Mark $\frac{1}{4}$) for 2 hours to dry. Store in an air-tight container.

Roasting Spread whole, blanched nuts in one layer on a baking tray. Place in a moderate oven (180°C, 350°F, Gas Mark 4) for 10–15 minutes. Shake and stir frequently. Remove from the oven when the nuts are an even, golden brown.

Grinding Blanch the nuts. Mix them with a little water and sugar and pass through a fine mincer. Alternatively, pound in a mortar with a little sugar. If you have a liquidiser, put 100 g (4 oz) nuts in the machine at a time, and grind at top speed.

Salting Melt 100 g (4 oz) butter with 4 tablespoons oil in a large frying pan. Add the nuts and sauté over a moderate heat, turning frequently with a slotted spoon. When golden brown, remove and spread on kitchen paper. Sprinkle with salt while they are still warm, making sure they are well coated.

O

Oatmeal

The oat is one of the seven major grains, and has been used for centuries in the form of oatmeal. Oatmeal is the whole grain, rolled or cut into flakes, and it is this minimal processing without refining, which makes it very valuable nutritionally.

Oatmeal marketed as 'instant' or 'quick cook' has usually been preheated before being rolled. The larger, flaked oatmeal, often called jumbo oats, takes longer to cook but has generally retained more of its nutritional value.

Oatmeal contains almost 17% protein, is a rich source of inositol and has more vitamin B_1 than any other breakfast cereal. It is rich in iron and phosphorus and has traces of copper, manganese, zinc and potassium.

There are three basic types of oatmeal; quick cook or rolled, which generally has small flakes; hulled or gritted oatmeal, and steel cut oatmeal. Steel cut oats have not undergone high temperatures, and hulled or gritted oatmeal has not been heated at all, so these two are considered nutritionally superior.

Uses Oatmeal is generally used for porridge or muesli (see page 70), but can be made into oatcakes or added to bread, cakes and biscuits.

Storage Store in a cool, dry place in an air-tight container.

Oils

Oils are one of the essentials of our diet. They contain lecithin, vitamins A, E and K, and minerals. When digested, fats and oils are broken down into glycerol and fatty acids. The body can manufacture all of the fatty acids it needs except linoleic, arachidic and linolenic acids from sugar. These three acids are therefore called the essential fatty acids.

The interest in oils over the last few years is, however, mainly in polyunsaturated fats, which have become popular due to their low cholesterol content, and saturated fats, which, in excess, can be damaging to health. As it happens, most animal fats are high in saturated fatty acids, and most vegetable fats are higher in polyunsaturated fats.

The current preoccupation with fats in the diet is the result of a fearful increase in deaths, in the last 25 years in many parts of the West, from what is loosely called heart disease. Many explanations have been offered, among them smoking, obesity, high blood pressure, lack of exercise, heredity, stress and the diet. In the diet, the main villains are considered to be any excess of sugar or saturated fats, or a combination of both.

Experts often disagree about the main causal factor, but there is statistical evidence to show that heart attacks are associated with a high level of blood fats – triglycerides and cholesterol, and the accumulation of fats on the inner walls of the blood vessels. Saturated fats, the solid type, increase the level of cholesterol and triglycerides in the blood and lead to deposits in the arteries. Polyunsaturated fats, the soft fats or oils of fish and vegetables, cause blood cholesterol to fall. Hence the advice to eat more fats which are completely unsaturated and fewer saturated fats.

It is impossible to eat only fat that is completely unsaturated, because all fat includes both saturated and unsaturated fatty acids, and it is the proportions of each that vary. The widely quoted recommendation of the American Heart Association to people with a high level of blood fats, is that the total amount of fat in the diet should not account for more than 35% of the individual's energy intake, and that the saturated fats should constitute less than 10%.

Many vegetable oils are used in cooking, but some are lower in cholesterol than others. They can be rated according to their richness in linoleic acid, a poly-unsaturated fatty acid.

Safflower oil, bland and almost without odour, has, for example, about 80% linoleic acid. Coconut oil, on the other hand, has only 2% and is heavily saturated.

Basically, oil is available in three conditions – cold pressed, semi-refined and refined. The simplest method of making oil is to take seeds and press them in a hydraulic press. This gives cold or first-press oil, also known as unrefined oil. It is rich in nutrients, colour and flavour, but tends to be expensive since so little oil is obtained from one pressing.

Semi-refined oil is made by cooking or heating the material and using continuous pressure at high temperatures. Many of the nutrients, especially vitamins, are lost and some discoloration takes place.

The third process is to extract the oil by dissolving the material in a petroleum based material. This method produces the most oil from the seeds and is the most popular with manufacturers. The oil produced is then purified with caustic soda and fuller's earth and preservatives are added to replace the natural anti-oxidants which have been lost during refining.

Most wholefood or health food shops sell semi-refined oils, but some may also sell unrefined oils. They are much cheaper but can play a very important part in the diet, since they contain many ingredients essential to the body, which cannot be found in refined oil products.

Olive oil

Olive oil, containing about 10% linoleic acid, is rich in monounsaturated fatty acids, which do not contribute to heart disease. Its rich oleic acid content makes it completely digestible and it has been found to increase the absorption of the fat soluble vitamins A, D, E and K.

The oil is made from olives which are easy to press and release their oil without heat or chemical action.

Country of origin The sun-baked olive groves of the Mediterranean were the first source of olive oil, and today it is exported from the olive producing Mediterranean countries such as Spain, Italy and Greece.

Uses It is used mainly as a salad oil and cooking medium.

Cooking instructions Some nutritionists advise combining olive oil with one high in linoleic acid, such as safflower, to get a really beneficial salad and cooking oil.

Storage Store in a cool, dark place.

Olives

Pasta

There is a deep-seated tradition that Marco Polo introduced pasta to Italy after he had visited China. This is probably due to the similarity of pasta and noodles.

There are about 150 major varieties of pasta, cut in every imaginable shape. The most important pastas are macaroni, spaghetti, lasagne, canelloni, vermicelli, tagliatelli, tortellini and rigatoni.

Traditionally, pasta is made from durum wheat. The endosperm, or starchy layer, is ground into a fine flour. Eggs are sometimes added to the mixture, as too is spinach in some special varieties.

Wholemeal pasta, a favourite of the health food enthusiast, uses the entire grain in its production. As a result, it contains more vitamins and minerals than ordinary pasta.

Cooking instructions Allow 100 g (4 oz) pasta per person and always cook in plenty of boiling salted water, at least 1·15 litres (2 pints) per 100 g (4 oz) pasta. A teaspoon of vegetable oil, added during cooking, will stop the pieces of pasta from sticking to each other.

Pasta

Storage Store in a cool, dry place in a covered container.

Peanut

Not true nuts, peanuts are actually the pods of a leguminous plant. The nuts grow on long tendrils below the ground, hence their alternative name 'ground nuts'. Two kernels grow in each nut, which has a soft shell. Before using for cooking, the pinkish skin should be removed by blanching (see page 45).

Country of origin Peanuts originated in South America, where they have been found in tombs dating back to 950 B.C.

Peanut plant

Uses Peanuts may be eaten raw, roasted, fried or salted. They are used in cakes, biscuits, salads and with vegetables, meat, poultry, fish and rice, as well as being a cocktail savoury and sandwich spread in the form of peanut butter. Peanuts are also used commercially to make peanut or groundnut oil (see below).

Cooking instructions Peanuts may be roasted, salted or ground (see page 45).
   To make peanut butter, put 1 cup of shelled peanuts into a liquidiser with 1–2 teaspoons oil and a pinch of salt. Grind until crunchy or smooth, according to taste.

Storage Store in a sealed container in a cool, dry place.

Peanut

Peanut oil

It is also known as arachis, or ground nut oil. Peanut oil has a high oleic acid content, up to 60%, and about 35% linoleic acid. It is non-drying and will keep liquid at room temperature.

Country of origin Peanut oil comes mainly from the U.S.A.

Uses Peanut oil which has been deodorised, as has most which is on sale, is bland in taste and so does not impart any specific taste to foods. It does not cloud over like some oils, and therefore may be clarified and used time and time again.

Storage Store in a cool, dry place.

Pearl barley See *Barley* (page 16).

Pearl millet See *Millet* (page 42).

Pecan nut

A smooth, oblong, thin-shelled nut, native to the southern part of the United States, pecan nuts are the fruit of the *Carya* family of trees. The shelled nuts, which resemble walnut kernels, are becoming increasingly popular for dessert use.

Country of origin They are indigenous to the southern states of the U.S.A. and are cultivated commercially in Texas and Oklahoma.

Uses A popular ingredient in many American pies and flans, pecans can be used in the same way as the walnut.

Cooking instructions Remove the brittle reddish-brown shell and blanch before use in cooking (see page 45).

Storage Store in an air-tight container in a cool place.

Pecan nut

Pigeon pea

Also called the red gram, Angola pea or yellow dhal, they vary in colour, but are usually red, brown or yellow.

Country of origin The pigeon pea is probably native to Africa, but is now an important crop in most hot climates.

Uses The tender young pods with their convoluted shape are sometimes eaten as a green vegetable, but usually the seeds or peas are eaten after drying. They are used in stuffings, stews, pot-roasts and savoury dishes.

Cooking instructions After soaking (see page 18), cook for $1-1\frac{1}{2}$ hours.

Storage Pigeon peas will keep for several years if stored in an air-tight container in a cool place.

Pigeon peas

Pine nut

This is the edible seed or kernel from the cone of some species of pine tree, and is similar in taste to the almond.

Country of origin It is native to the semi-arid areas of south-western U.S.A. and Mexico but is now also found in Asia, Europe and around the Mediterranean.

Uses Chopped pine nuts are used in stuffings, meat recipes, aubergine dishes, sweet and sour sauces, rice mixtures and salads.

Pine nut

Cooking instructions These nuts, although they have a distinctive, pleasant taste, sometimes have a strong turpentine flavour. This disappears with long storing and 25% longer cooking (see page 45).

Storage Store in a ventilated container in a cool, dry place.

Pistachio nut

The pistachio is the fruit of the deciduous tree, *Bistacia Vera*, which is native to the Middle East. The nut is about the size of a small olive. The small, green kernel, encased in a thin, yellowish-red wrinkled skin, has a sweet, distinctive flavour. The kernel separates easily from its shell when the nut is broken open. Pistachios are sold both in their shells and shelled and blanched.

Country of origin Although native to the Middle East, they are now grown extensively in Asia, the Mediterranean and the warmer regions of the Americas.

Uses Pistachios are used extensively as a flavouring in meat cookery, pastry making and confectionery. Blanched and chopped, they can be used in making cakes and desserts. They are also added to stuffings and ice-cream and are incorporated into many savoury dishes, as well as being eaten as a dessert nut.

Pistachio nut

Cooking instructions Pistachios can be fried and salted (see page 45). To preserve the brilliant green colour of the nut for cooking purposes, blanch by covering with cold water and bringing to the boil. Strain and cover again with cold water. Remove the skins and dry slowly.

Storage Store in an air-tight and light-proof tin or green bottle to retain the green colour after drying.

Postum See *Coffee* (page 27).

Prosso See *Millet* (page 42).

Prunes

Prunes are made from plums with a high sugar content, which can be dried without removing the stone. They only have about half as much sugar as dates, figs and raisins, and only half as many calories.

Country of origin The U.S.A. is the major producer of prunes, made either by sun-drying, as in California, or by artificial heat. Most American varieties are of European origin.

Prune

51

Uses Prunes are eaten mainly as a dessert, either hot or cold, but may be used in cakes and confectionery. Their particular value often lies in their natural laxative properties. Prunes are available dried or canned in syrup.

Cooking instructions Soak dried prunes overnight, or for at least six hours, to reconstitute if required. Simply heat canned prunes for use, since they have already been cooked and soaked.

Storage Dried prunes can be stored in an air-tight container for up to six months. Canned prunes have a shelf life of up to one year.

Raisins

The best dessert raisins, which are large and sweet, are of the Malaga variety, which are dried 'Muscat grapes. They are more robust than sultanas and chewier than currants.

Country of origin Raisins are grown in many parts of the eastern Mediterranean, Australia and South Africa.

Uses Raisins make an excellent addition to muesli, cakes, biscuits, pastries, stuffings, meat dishes, rice mixtures, puddings and salads.

Raisins

Cooking instructions Wash carefully in hot water and dry before use, unless guaranteed unsprayed with mineral oil.

Storage Stored in an air-tight container, raisins will keep well for up to one year. Raisins also freeze well.

Rice

Rice has been a staple food for thousands of years in Asia, China, Africa, South America, Spain and Italy.

Rice has a similar structure to wheat, and when it is milled, the outer layers are removed and the valuable nutrients are lost.

Country of origin Most of our rice today comes from China, Pakistan and India.

Rice

Uses Rice is used as a cooked cereal-type dish, and as a cooked grain to be eaten with meat, fish and vegetables.

Use in rice mixtures with vegetables and for puddings and cakes.

There are seven main types of rice on the market:–

Brown rice Here only the indigestible husks have been removed.

Brown rice

White rice Here the husk, germ and outer layers have been removed. Often the grains are polished with glucose or talc to give a gleaming white appearance. This process takes away much of the protein, B vitamins and most of the minerals from the rice.

Rice flakes This is processed rice which has been power-flaked for quick and easy cooking.

Converted rice Here the unmilled grain is treated with steam under pressure, which forces the vitamins to be carried to the centre of the grain. It can then be milled without any loss of vitamin nutrients.

Rice polish This is the bran which is removed when the rice is milled. It is a very good source of vitamin B and can be worked into biscuits, pancakes etc., and used as a meal stretcher with meat, fish or poultry.

Rice flour This is made from the by-products of the milling process, including some bran, ground into a fine flour. It is rich in B vitamins.

Wild rice Wild rice was grown for centuries by the North American Indians and is now grown commercially, often in artificial ponds. Wild rice is very expensive and is nutritionally very superior.

Cooking instructions Rice should be cooked so that the grains remain separate. A very simple method is to allow $1\frac{1}{2}$ cups of water to each cup of rice (brown and whole grain rice need two cups of water). Bring to the boil, add a pinch of salt, and immediately reduce the heat to a very low simmer. Cover with a tight-fitting lid. Cook for about 20–40 minutes until all the water is absorbed. Brown rice will take a longer time to cook than white rice.

Storage Store in a cool, dry place in a covered container for up to six months.

Wild rice

Rose cocoa bean See *Beans* (page 17).

Rye

To the Ancient Greeks, rye was merely a weed, and it was not until the time of the Roman Empire that rye was planted as a crop. By the Middle Ages, rye had become the staple grain throughout Europe, and the basic loaf in England was made from roughly ground rye and barley. In Eastern Europe, especially Germany, rye has still retained its popularity and both the Russians and the Scandinavians prefer the flavour of dark rye bread.

Rye is nutritionally very sound too, with 12% protein and a very good proportion of vitamins and minerals.

There are two basic rye products for use by health food lovers:–

Rye flour This is low in gluten, so bread made from all rye will rise less and be flatter than that made with high gluten grains such as wheat. It is however, very filling and has a good flavour. Rye flour packets are often labelled 'dark' or 'light'. The light flour has been sifted and contains less bran.

Rye groats These are the whole grains of rye.

Uses It is a delicious addition to fresh vegetables and salads in whole grain form. The flour is delicious when made into rye bread and sweet tea breads. Rye groats may be soaked and cooked like rice, or cracked with a rolling pin for shorter cooking.

Cooking instructions After soaking the groats – about 1 hour, cook in boiling salted water for about 20 minutes or until tender.

Rye

Storage Both groats and flour should be stored in an airtight container in a cool, dry place.

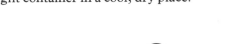

Safflower oil

Oil from the safflower, a member of the *Compositae* family. Safflower oil has the highest linoleic acid content of all oils, having up to 80%.

Country of origin Safflowers were cultivated by ancient civilisations along the Nile and south into Ethiopia. The Arabs have also adopted the cultivation of this tall, thistle-like flower.

Safflower plant

Uses It is used as a salad oil and cooking medium. Recent tests in the U.S.A. have shown that safflower, and other oils high in linoleic acid, tend to lower the cholesterol level in the blood (although vitamins B and E were also needed to maintain low blood cholesterol).

Storage Store in a cool, dry place.

Safflower seed

Salt

Salt is a fundamental substance, important to all animal life, since it keeps the body's fluids in balance. As such it is a mineral essential for life. It is also valued for its preservative and disinfectant properties. It is therefore often used for sterilising materials and equipment.

The individual requirements for salt can largely be worked out by common sense, but according to the Manual of Nutrition, the amount of salt needed each day is about 4 g in a temperate climate. A person living in a very hot climate, or doing very heavy work, causing him to perspire, will obviously need more salt than one in a temperate climate or sitting behind an office desk.

The following types of salt are available :–

Table salt Usually water is pumped into underground salt mines and the resulting brine is vacuum dried. Table salt is ground finely and often starch, phosphate of lime and other substances are added for smooth flowing.

Rock salt This is another name for land salt, as it occurs in rock veins below the ground.

Crystal salt Such salt is obtained by evaporating sea water in enclosed areas. It has a distinctive flavour and is recommended by several health experts because it has a high iodine content.

Iodised salt Generally this is table salt to which potassium has been added. Leading nutritionists recommend this for regular use.
Storage Salt will keep indefinitely in a cool, dry place.

Seaweed See *Kelp* (page 39).

Sea salt See *Salt* (page 55).

Sesame oil

Also known as gingelly or benne oil, it is the oil extracted from sesame seeds. It contains about 40% linoleic acid and 50% oleic acid, plus a good proportion of lecithin.

55

Country of origin Sesame oil has been used for cooking in Africa and the Far East for many centuries.

Uses Use as a salad oil and cooking medium.

Cooking instructions The main advantage of sesame oil over other oils is that it does not turn rancid, even in hot weather. Analysis has revealed that an ingredient, sesamol, is responsible for keeping the oil stable and free from rancidity. This substance is added to all margarines by law in Sweden.

Storage Store in a cool, dry place.

Sesame seeds

In Hindu mythology, the God Yama blessed the sesame seed and it has since come to be regarded throughout the East as a symbol of immortality.

Sesame seeds come from the attractive sesame plant. The seeds are packed with vitamins and minerals, calcium, iron and protein.

Both Turkey and the Arab countries use sesame seeds to make a creamy paste called tahini, which forms part of their staple diet. Another favourite is halva which is a sweet made from seasame seeds.

Sesame seeds

Country of origin Sesame seeds came originally from Turkey and the Arab countries.

Uses It is often used as a crunchy topping for breads, and is added to cakes and biscuits for its nutritive value. It is also an interesting ingredient in salads.

Storage Store in a cool, dry place in an air-tight container.

Shallu See *Sorghum* (page 56).

Sorghum

This is an extremely hardy, drought-withstanding grain which gradually became the staple food in hot, dry countries and is still the major cereal grain throughout Africa today. The Chinese and Japanese also eat it and cook it the same way as rice.

Country of origin Sorghum was first grown in Africa and India.

Several types of sorghum are available on the market :–

Kafir This is a native to South Africa, it is also called

Kafir corn. It has smallish seeds, varying in colour from white through pink to red.

Milo From Eastern Africa, it has larger seeds of a salmon or pink colour.

Feteritas This variety comes from the Sudan and has very large, white seeds.

Shallu From India, but also known as Egyptian wheat, it has large white seed heads.

Sorghum flour This is gluten free, and so produces flattish bread. The whole sorghum grain is always ground into flour or meal. This ensures a high nutrient content, but poor keeping qualities. This flour must be kept under refrigeration, otherwise the oil in the embryo will go rancid.

Uses As a cooked grain it is used like rice with vegetables and also as a flour to make breads, cakes and biscuits. It is a very nutritious addition to stews and casseroles or soups.

Storage Store the grain in a cool, dry place. Keep the flour under refrigeration.

Sorghum

Soya bean

It is known also as the soy bean, haba soya and preta bean. This is the master of all beans as far as nutritional value is concerned, since it contains all eight essential amino acids, which the body cannot manufacture and, as such, is a complete protein.

There are many varieties of the soya bean, but they can be classified into two main types. The edible vegetable bean, and the commercial field species, which is used for soya bean oil, meal and flour.

Soya beans contain as much protein as top quality steak, but the difference is that they contain unsaturated fats. The iron in soya products is also of an assimilable form. Soya beans are also rich in most minerals and vitamins – although they contain only a moderate amount of vitamin A.

Country of origin The soya bean is native to China but has spread to Japan and Korea and is now a very valuable crop to the U.S.A.

Uses Soya products include flour, oil, milk, texturised vegetable protein and the traditionally fermented foods such as miso and tofu.

Soya bean plant

Soya beans

Soya products available from health food shops are:–

Soya grits The raw bean is broken into 8–10 pieces which cook in minutes rather than hours. They can be used in any recipe which calls for cooked soya beans.

Soya bean sprouts These are the sprouts of the dried soya bean, which produce their own vitamin C (see *Sprouting seeds* page 59).

Texturised vegetable protein This is soya, spun and textured to simulate meat. All TVP comes in easy-to-use mixtures. It is made from soya flour or soya protein concentrate, which is extruded into small chunks, bits or granules. The dried chunks can be reconstituted into main meal dishes such as meat sauces, casseroles and pie fillings or minced and added to beef as an extender.

Soya milk This milk is useful for vegans and for those who cannot drink cow's milk. It is sold canned, bottled or as a spray-dried powder. Soya milk is richer in iron than cow's milk but has less calcium, phosphorus and vitamin A.

Soya flour There are three types of soya flour generally available. Full fat flour, which contains 20% fat; medium fat flour, which contains 5–8% fat and fat free soya flour. It is important to know which flour is used, since the amount of liquid used in recipes will differ according to the type. Low fat or fat free flours require more liquid.

Soya flour contains no gluten, but can be safely added to bread recipes in the ratio of 2 tablespoons soya flour to 225 g (8 oz) wheat flour. Add the flour to soups, gravies and casseroles as an easy way to achieve the best protein balance for a meal.

Soya oil Soya oil is obtained from beans in two main ways – by the expeller process, in which a rotating shaft presses the cooked beans, and by the solvent process, where chemicals are used to extract the oil. Most suppliers to the health food industry would not use this latter method. Soya oil is rich in lecithin and linoleic acid. It is used in cooking, margarines, cakes, pastries, doughs, soups and sweet making. The oil should be stored in a cool, dark place.

Fermented soya bean products A good deal of ingenuity goes into producing fermented soya bean products such as soy sauce, tempeh, miso and tofu.

Soy sauce Here the cooked beans are mixed with roasted wheat and treated with the micro-organism *Aspergillus Oryzae*. Salt is added to quicken the growth of the fungus. The mixture is allowed to ferment from six months to five years. During this time, the vats are stirred twice a day. When the beans are ready, the liquid should be a rich, dense brown. This is strained off and bottled and the residues are used as a fertiliser. It is used to flavour foods such as rice, meat and fish and can be used in much the same way as Worcestershire sauce.

Tempeh This is a sort of cheese made from fermented soya beans. It is best compared to Gorgonzola cheese because of its strong taste and smell.

Miso This is a soya bean paste which can be mixed into soups, spreads and gravies or used like a yeast extract to enhance the flavour of a casserole. Vegetables marinated in miso paste make an excellent home-made pickle.

Tofu This is a soya bean curd with a soft, delicate texture and pale colour, which is sold in slabs or slices. The fresh curd should always be kept refrigerated. The bean curd can be fermented to make cheese and the result is a highly flavoured cheese known in China as 'chou tofu' – or stinking curd. It is slightly thicker than cottage cheese, for which it can be substituted in every recipe.

Cooking instructions Rinse the beans well and soak for 24 hours. The bean will double in size during soaking, so allow at least three times the amount of water. Change the water, bring the beans to the boil and simmer for 2–4 hours. Add any seasonings during the last hour of cooking, but do not add salt until just before serving.

Sprouting seeds

These are known as bean sprouts and grain sprouts. To many people, sprouting beans mean sprouting mung beans, but almost any whole seed is capable of sprouting. Sprouts are often produced from grains such as wheat, barley, maize, corn, oats and legumes such as soya beans, mung beans, lima beans, alfalfa beans, chick peas, lentils, fenugreek and navy beans.

All bean sprouts are nutritionally very valuable. They are especially rich in vitamin C and several of the B complex vitamins. They also contain a higher level of protein and amino acids than most vegetables. Some sprouts are also a good source of vitamins E, G, K and U.

Sprouting seeds

59

*Sprouting
seeds in a jar*

Legumes generally have a higher level of vitamin C than grains, but grains contain more vitamin B.

How to sprout There are several sprouting utensils on the market, but by far the simplest way is to use a glass jar. Place the dried seeds inside the jar, cover with muslin or cheesecloth and secure with a rubber band. Rinse several times a day with warm water and leave the jar on its side to drain. Choose a large jar, since the beans or grains usually expand to ten times their original size. To get off to a quick start, flood the seeds with water for several hours to swell them.

Some seeds take a longer time to sprout, but the longest time is about six days. Keep the beans in a warm place, but not in direct sunlight. Always use whole seeds. Split peas, cracked wheat and husked rice will not sprout.

Cooking instructions Steaming or stir-frying preserves the vitamins in the bean sprouts and generally makes them taste better than boiling. If cooking with other vegetables, the bean sprouts should only be added for the last couple of minutes of cooking time.

Storage Sprouted seeds will keep in the refrigerator for up to four days.

Stoneground wholemeal flour See *Wheat* (page 63).

Sultanas

Sultanas are the dried version of the white, seedless sultana grape. They taste softer and sweeter than currants or raisins.

Country of origin Sultanas are grown in many parts of the eastern Mediterranean, Australia and South Africa, although the best varieties come from Turkey.

Sultanas

Uses Sultanas are used in cakes, biscuits, desserts, muesli, pastries, salads and as a sweet ingredient in meat and savoury dishes.

Cooking instructions Wash carefully in hot water and dry before use, unless guaranteed unsprayed with mineral oil.

Storage Stored in an air-tight container, sultanas will keep well for up to one year. Sultanas also freeze well.

Sunflower oil

The oil from the sunflower has a high linoleic acid content – second only to safflower oil, it contains 65%. Almost half of the sunflower seed is made up of molecules of oil. It also contains oleic and palmitic acids. Sunflower oil is rich in vitamins E, A and D.

Country of origin Sunflower oil comes mainly from Africa and Russia.

Uses It is used as a salad oil and cooking medium and also as a diuretic, and so benefits some kidney complaints. It can also limit the risk of disorders from cholesterol deposits in the blood vessels.

Storage Store in a cool, dry place.

Sunflower seeds

The North American Indians appreciated the medicinal value of the sunflower and they cultivated large crops of it. In Russia today, sunflowers are a multi-million rouble crop and extensive use is made of the oil from the seeds.

Sunflower seeds are remarkably rich in B complex vitamins and are a good source of phosphorus, magnesium, iron, calcium, potassium, protein and vitamin E.

Sunflower seeds also contain many trace elements such as zinc, manganese, copper and carotene.

Country of origin Most of the crop of sunflower seeds comes from the U.S.A. and Russia.

Uses Use sunflower seeds for topping breads; add to salads and vegetables for an interesting flavour and texture. Sunflowers are also used for making the following products :–

Sunflower oil (see above).

Sunflower meal When the sunflower seeds are crushed to make oil, the 'defatted meat' of the seed which is left is called the meal. It is very nutritious and although, at one time, was only used for animal feed, today is sold in many health food stores.

Storage Store in a cool, dry place in an air-tight container for up to six months.

Sunflower

Sunflower seeds

Sweet corn See *Corn* (page 29).

61

T

Tea See *Herbal teas* (page 36).

Tempeh See *Soya bean* (page 57).

Texturised vegetable protein See *Soya bean* (page 57).

Tofu See *Soya bean* (page 57).

Triticale

This is a cross bred grain, produced by crossing wheat with rye. The result is a grain with 2% more protein than either wheat or rye and with a better amino acid balance than wheat.

Country of origin It is grown throughout northern U.S.A., Canada and Russia as well as the U.K.

Uses Use as wheat (see page 63).

Cooking instructions Triticale flour makes an excellent bread, but remember to handle the dough as little as possible and use smooth, gentle kneading, since it contains a softer, lighter gluten than wheat flour.

Storage Store in a cool, dry place in a closed container.

W

Wakame See *Kelp* (page 39).

Walnut

Walnut

The walnut is the fruit of the walnut tree, which is thought to have originated in ancient Persia or China. Like most nuts, the walnut has a smooth, outer green husk which is removed when the ripe nuts are picked and sold. The outer shell is removed and only the kernel is eaten. However, one of the most delicious forms of walnut is the pickled unripe nut, which is harvested while the kernel, shell and husk are still soft.

Country of origin Walnuts originated in ancient Persia or China and are now cultivated throughout Europe.

Uses Walnuts are used extensively in every form of cooking, in soups and sauces, stuffings and garnishings, desserts and puddings and as a valuable ingredient for winter salads. The unripe fruit, as well as being pickled, can also be made into a chutney.

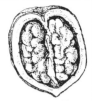

Cooking instructions To pickle walnuts, immerse in a spiced brine after pricking with a fork. Leave immersed for about a week. Drain and place in the light for about a week, turning once or twice, so that they become blackened all over. Return to the jars with spiced vinegar. Use within two months.

Storage Store in an air-tight container in a cool place.

Open walnut

Water

There are several types of water available on the market but the three main types are :–

Bottled water This can be defined as 'water which is sealed in bottles or other containers and intended for human consumption'. It is very distinct from mineral waters which come from spring sources. There is also no guarantee that the water is free from chlorine. It is really a question of checking the label.

Distilled water This is pure H_2O, which is free from any bacteria and also free from minerals. It also has a very flat taste.

Mineral waters These are recognised sources of many beneficial minerals. They can be positively health giving, since they come from the many natural springs which contain calcium, iron and other trace minerals. Medicinal claims have been made for these waters, and it is probable that they aid digestion and help stomach troubles.

Wheat

Wheat is commonly known as the universal grain; half the population of the world relies upon it to provide a staple food.

Country of origin The first wheat began to grow at least 10,000 years ago in the fertile crescent surrounding the Eastern Mediterranean. Hardy and truly versatile, it has grown and flourished in every climate. Our wheat comes mainly from the U.S.A., Canada and Russia.

*Durum
wheat*

Types of Wheat The many varieties can basically be divided into hard and soft wheat. British wheat is generally soft and American wheat, hard. Hard wheat contains more gluten and is better for baking bread. Soft wheat is good for baking cakes and biscuits. Flour manufacturers often combine wheat from both countries to get a good mixture. Hard grain flour is usually sold as 'strong flour'.

Durum wheat This has amber coloured grains and is used exclusively in pasta products.

White wheat This is low in protein and very starchy. It is used mainly in pastries and breakfast cereals.

Hard red winter wheat This has been developed in Canada and takes only 90 days between sowing and harvesting. It is very good for making bread.

Maris dove is the most common British wheat. It is a soft, winter wheat and is high in protein.

Kibbled wheat Here, the whole wheat grains are cracked in a machine called a kibbler, so that they are broken into small pieces, rather than being milled. It is used in bread making and in cereals.

Cracked wheat Here the whole wheat grain is cracked by pressure machinery. Splitting the grain ensures that it cooks faster and yet retains the nutritional value of the wheat.

Wheat flakes Whole wheat grains can be rolled to produce wheat flakes, their advantage being that they can be more easily cooked than in their whole form.

Muesli is made using wheat flakes with other flaked grains, nuts, fruit and sugar if liked, but wheat flakes may also be used as a topping for pies and casseroles or in biscuits and bread.

The following flours are generally available :–

Wholemeal flour This contains all the wheat grain, including the bran and wheat germ. It is much coarser in texture than other flours and higher in nutritional value. Wholemeal flour is only permitted to have one additive – caramel. Wholemeal (or wholewheat) bread may contain, with the exception of bleach, all the additives found in white bread.

Stoneground wholemeal flour This is a flour in which the germ is evenly distributed by being milled at slow speeds between stones at low temperatures.

White flour Wheat flour has been whitened for centuries, ever since the Middle Ages, when it was associated with purity. White flour is made from the starchy endosperm of the wheat grain. In the milling process 35% of the grain, bran and surface endosperm is removed, leaving creamy granules. These are then bleached with chlorine dioxide. Modern flours are enriched with certain vitamins and minerals.

81% or 85% extraction flour This is usually sold as wheatmeal flour. The miller is aiming at a finer flour by extracting the coarser parts. Sieving 19% of the ground grain removes the bran and some of the aleurone layer. Depending upon the variety of grain, the coarse extraction will take out between 15 and 19% of the grain. Extraction wheatmeal flour does not contain bran.

Storage All flours should be stored in a cool, dry place.

Wheatgerm

In the germ, or kernel, of the wheat is a tiny embryo which contains all the nutrients needed for the future life of the wheat grain. Before the introduction of the steel roller flour-milling process in 1879, the wheat was crushed between two flat stones and so the complete wheat was eaten. Today the wheatgerm is removed during the making of white flour.

Wheatgerm is particularly rich in the B complex vitamins and vitamin E. It is a good source of iron and calcium and contains 12 amino acids, which build up to produce a good protein.

Wheatgerm can be bought from health food shops in three forms: as natural wheatgerm, or as stabilised wheatgerm, where the product has been treated to overcome the problems of rancidity, but at the expense of the more fragile constituents. It will state clearly on the pack if the wheatgerm has been stabilised. Finally, it is available as wheatgerm oil, which is often taken as a supplement to the diet.

Uses Wheatgerm is delicious added to a cereal with yogurt or in muesli. It can also be added to any bread recipe – a good proportion is 50 g (2 oz) wheatgerm to 400 g (14 oz) flour. A higher proportion of wheatgerm will need extra moisture.

Added to meat loaves and patties, it improves the flavour and nutritional content. Mix with granola for fruit crumbles, or add a knob of butter and cheese and use for a casserole topping. Wheatgerm can also be

Common wheat

Wheatgerm

added to stuffings or used instead of breadcrumbs when coating meat, fish and vegetables.

Storage Natural wheatgerm is highly perishable and must be kept under refrigeration.

White flour See *Wheat* (page 63).

White rice See *Rice* (page 52).

Wild rice See *Rice* (page 52).

Wholemeal flour See *Wheat* (page 63).

Wholemeal pasta See *Pasta* (page 48).

𝒴

Yeast extracts

When fresh brewer's yeast (see page 22) is mixed with salt, it is broken down by its own enzymes. The soluble residue is evaporated under pressure to give the familiar sticky brown substance, known as yeast extract. These extracts are also known as hydrolysed or autolysed yeasts.

Yeast extracts are particularly rich in B vitamins and many of the yeast extracts aimed at the vegetarian market contain vegetable protein, iron and added vitamin B_{12}.

Uses They can be quickly and easily dissolved in water to make an excellent stock or a warming drink. A spoonful will also give body to a stew or casserole. It also makes an nutritious snack spread thinly on wholemeal bread or crackers. These extracts can have a very high salt content, so take in moderation and feed to young infants from time to time only.

Storage Yeast extracts are usually sold in handy jars. Keep the lid screwed on well and store in a cool, dry place for up to six months.

Yogurt

According to an ancient tradition, an angel revealed to the prophet Abraham the method of making yogurt. The Bible tells us he lived to be 175 and fathered a child when he was 100. This is probably the origin of the idea that yogurt is associated with longevity and fertility, and the debate continues to this day.

What is known however, is that yogurt does produce an environment in the intestine which is unfavourable to harmful bacteria. This is an important factor when so many modern drugs can destroy the normal valuable intestinal bacteria. Yogurt must be taken regularly to produce this sort of environment.

Much of the commercial yogurt on sale today contains preservatives and colouring but it is very easy and cheap to make your own.

Home-made yogurt Bring 600 ml (1 pint) milk to the boil and hold for about 5 seconds. Let it cool down to 43°C (110°F), just above body temperature, so that it feels comfortable when tested with a clean finger. Pour the milk into a flask. Stir in 2 tablespoons of live yogurt and leave to thicken. With the top on the flask it will take between 3 and 8 hours. Refrigerate as soon as it has thickened, but do not shake, as this causes curds to form. Mix with honey for breakfast, serve with meat, curries and casseroles or as a dessert with fruit.

Recipes

*The best diet for health
is one with a balance of necessary
nutrients. But eating a well-balanced diet
should mean more than just consuming a daily
ration of vitamins, proteins and other essentials.
It can, and should, be thoroughly enjoyable.
Here are lots of recipes for tasty
ways with wholefood cereals, fruit, eggs, cheese,
yogurt and nuts to suit every occasion, and
mouthwatering all-vegetable dishes to tempt everyone.
Healthy eating is not dull eating –
try these recipes for proof.*

Guide to using Recipes

All the recipes in this book have a protein, calorie and cholesterol rating as follows:

Protein The average adult needs 85 g (3 oz) protein per day. The guide refers to the following values:

◆ When one portion of the recipe contains over 20 g protein.

◈ When one portion of the recipe contains over 10 g protein.

◇ When one portion of the recipe contains less than 10 g protein.

Calories All food contains calories, but in order to achieve the balance between the energy our food contains, and the energy our body uses up, it is important to calculate the calorific value of each recipe. The guide used here refers to the following values:

○ When one portion of the recipe contains under 200 calories.

◑ When one portion of the recipe contains between 200 and 400 calories.

● When one portion of the recipe contains over 400 calories.

Remember the calorific value given refers only to one portion; additional servings mean more calories.

Cholesterol This is a fatty substance which, in moderation, is essential for good health, but in high proportions has been found to be one of the contributory factors leading to heart disease. It is found in saturated animal fats such as butter, cream, milk, hard cheeses, lamb, beef and also in coconut oil. These should generally be replaced, in a low cholesterol diet, with polyunsaturated fats, found principally in vegetable foods and oils. The cholesterol guide here refers to the following values:

 Eat as often as you like, providing you are not trying to lose weight. They contain very little cholesterol per portion.

 Eat in moderation – one portion of this recipe will contain a small amount of saturated fat.

 Avoid eating this recipe or eat it very infrequently, since it has a high proportion of animal fats compared to polyunsaturated fats.

Calorie and Cholesterol Chart

Calories

High	Medium	Low
butter, lard, margarines, oils, cream cheese, cream, hard cheese, whole milk, chocolate, manufactured baked goods, nuts, avocado pears, olives, oily fish, pork, mutton, alcohol.	lamb, beef, ham, sausages, canned meats, salad dressings, cornflour, low calorie fats.	white fish, shellfish, skimmed milk, eggs, cottage cheese, low fat yogurt, most fruit and vegetables, low calorie dressings, low calorie drinks, low calorie breads.

Cholesterol

High	Medium	Low
lard, butter, non-polyunsaturated margarines, vegetable oils, white fats, cream cheese, cream, whole milk, tongue, offal, most shellfish, cod's roe, cashew nuts, chocolate, dairy ice cream, manufactured baked goods	olive oil, hard cheese, coffee creamers, whole eggs, coconut, beef, bacon, pork, lamb, ham, sausages, canned meats, avocado pears, olives, oily fish, canned fish.	all fruit and vegetables, corn oil, polyunsaturated margarines, sunflower seed oil, safflower oil, cottage cheese, low fat yogurt, skimmed milk, egg whites, most nuts, chicken, turkey, white fish, lobster, textured vegetable protein, sugar, jams, jellies, honey, flour, bread, breakfast cereals, pasta, rice, coffee, tea, alcohol, salt, spices.

Breakfast Dishes

Honey and Orange Vitaliser

juice of 2 oranges
1 egg yolk
1 teaspoon honey

Pour the orange juice into a jug and beat in the egg yolk and the honey. Alternatively, place in a liquidiser and mix at high speed for 30 seconds. *Serves 1*

Apple Muesli with Yogurt

2 dessert apples
2 tablespoons lemon juice
1 (142-ml/5-fl oz) carton natural
yogurt
2 tablespoons honey
6 tablespoons water
100 g (4 oz) mixed grains
2 tablespoons chopped hazelnuts or
almonds

Core the apples and peel if liked. Chop finely and place in a basin. Pour over the lemon juice and mix well to prevent the apples from browning. Add the yogurt, honey and water, mix well, then stir in the mixed grains. Serve sprinkled with chopped nuts. *Serves 4*

Almond Crunch Granola

Cooking time 20–25 minutes

225 g (8 oz) blanched almonds
450 g (1 lb) rolled oats
8 tablespoons clear honey
2 tablespoons safflower oil
1 teaspoon vanilla essence

Coarsely chop the almonds and mix with the rolled oats. Stir in the honey, safflower oil and vanilla essence. Mix well, then spread the mixture thinly over two lightly greased baking trays.

Bake in a moderate oven (180°C, 350°F, Gas Mark 4) for 20–25 minutes, turning occasionally, so that the oats are evenly browned. Cool, then store in sealed jars or containers for up to 1 month. Serve with milk and fresh or dried fruit. *Makes 12 servings*

Apple Muffins

Cooking time 15–20 minutes

65 g (2½ oz) butter, melted
225 g (8 oz) flour
½ teaspoon salt
2 teaspoons baking powder
50 g (2 oz) raw cane sugar
½ teaspoon ground cinnamon
¼ teaspoon grated nutmeg
¼ teaspoon ground allspice
2 eggs
150 ml (¼ pint) buttermilk
1 tablespoon lemon juice
2 medium dessert apples, peeled, cored
and grated

◇ ◗ ♥

Generously grease a muffin pan with 15 g (½ oz) of the butter, and set aside.

Sift the flour, salt, baking powder, sugar, cinnamon, nutmeg and allspice into a large mixing bowl and set aside.

In a mixing bowl, beat the eggs until pale yellow in colour. Add the remaining butter, the buttermilk and lemon juice to the eggs and stir well.

Stir the egg and flour mixtures together as quickly as possible. Do not over mix. Fold in the grated apples.

Spoon the batter into the prepared muffin pan. Bake in the centre of a very hot oven (230°C, 450°F, Gas Mark 8) for 15–20 minutes, or until a skewer inserted in the centre comes out clean. Remove from the oven, allow to cool slightly in the pan before serving warm. *Makes 12*
Note Although apples have been used in this recipe, any other fruit may be substituted, such as blackberries, apricots, plums, blueberries, raspberries etc.

Soups and Starters

Basic Vegetable Stock
Cooking time 30 minutes

2 tablespoons oil
175g (6 oz) unpeeled turnips, chopped
2 medium onions, peeled and chopped
4 sticks celery, chopped
1·5 litres (2¾ pints) water
2 teaspoons salt
1 bouquet garni
3 black peppercorns

◇ ○ ♡

To make dark vegetable stock Add to the basic stock ingredients 4 medium carrots, left unpeeled and chopped, 100 g (4 oz) mushrooms, wiped clean and chopped and 100 g (4 oz) tomatoes, quartered.
To make light vegetable stock Add to the basic stock ingredients 175 g (6 oz) parsnips, left unpeeled and chopped and 4 tablespoons mushroom stalks.

Prepare the vegetables according to which stock you are making.

Heat the oil over a moderate heat in a large saucepan. Add all the vegetables to the pan and fry, stirring occasionally for 5–7 minutes for light stock, 8–10 minutes for dark stock. Do not brown the vegetables for light stock.

Pour the water into the pan and add the salt, bouquet garni and peppercorns. Bring to the boil, stirring occasionally. Reduce the heat and simmer for 30 minutes.

Strain the stock into a bowl, pressing the vegetables with the back of a spoon to extract as many of the juices as possible. Remove the vegetables, bouquet garni and peppercorns.

Cool to room temperature then cover and store in the refrigerator until required. *Makes 1·4 litres (2½ pints)*

Split Pea Soup with Mint and Tomatoes

Cooking time 1¼ hours

25 g (1 oz) butter
1 onion, peeled and chopped
*4 tomatoes, peeled, seeds removed and
chopped*
*225 g (8 oz) split peas, soaked overnight
and drained*
250 ml (8 fl oz) stock
250 ml (8 fl oz) water
2 tablespoons chopped mint
salt and freshly ground black pepper
½ teaspoon dried basil
*1 tomato, peeled, seeds removed and cut
into strips*
½ teaspoon chopped mint

Melt the butter in a large saucepan and add the onion.
Cook, stirring occasionally, until the onion is soft but
not coloured. Add the tomatoes and split peas and stir to
coat with butter. Pour in the stock and water. Stir in the
mint, salt, pepper and basil. Bring the soup to the boil,
stirring constantly. Cover the pan and simmer the soup
for 1½ hours, or until the peas are very soft. Rub the soup
through a sieve into a large mixing bowl, adding the
contents of the sieve. Alternatively, purée in a liquidiser
until smooth.

Return the puréed soup to a clean pan. If necessary,
thin with a little extra stock. Bring to the boil, stirring
constantly. Serve the soup in warmed, individual
serving bowls, garnished with the tomato strips and
chopped mint. *Serves 4*

Split Pea Rasam
Cooking time 1¼ hours

225 g (8 oz) split peas, soaked overnight
finely grated rind and juice of 2 medium
oranges
salt and freshly ground black pepper
4 tablespoons oil
225 g (8 oz) onion, peeled and finely
chopped
¼ teaspoon ground cumin
½ teaspoon ground turmeric
2 teaspoons ground coriander
chopped chives

◗ ◖ ♡

Drain the water from the peas and make up to 1·75 litres (3 pints) with water. Simmer the peas in a covered pan in this liquid with the orange rind and a good pinch of salt. Cook until tender – about 1 hour. Cool a little, then purée in a liquidiser or pass through a fine sieve.

Heat the oil in a large saucepan and fry the onion to a golden brown. Stir in the cumin, turmeric and coriander and cook gently for 1 minute. Pour in the pea purée, season and bring to the boil. Cover and simmer for 10–15 minutes.

Stir in the orange juice, adjust the seasoning and garnish with scissored chives. Serve with hunks of wholemeal bread. *Serves 6*

Coriander Mushrooms
Cooking time 5 minutes

225 g (8 oz) small button mushrooms
6 tablespoons olive oil
1 teaspoon crushed coriander seeds
2 tablespoons lemon juice
sea salt and freshly ground black pepper
chopped parsley

◇ ○ ♡

Wipe the mushrooms with a damp cloth and cut them into halves or quarters.

Heat 4 tablespoons of the oil in a large frying pan. Add the coriander seeds and fry for about 2 minutes, stirring. Add the mushrooms and stir well. Cover and cook for 3–5 minutes until tender.

Remove from the heat and transfer the mushrooms and any liquid to a bowl. Add the remaining oil and lemon juice and season to taste. Allow to cool then chill before serving.

Serve in small bowls, sprinkled with chopped parsley. Buttered wholewheat bread makes this a more substantial dish. *Serves 2*

Creamy Avocado Pâté

2 avocados
4 eggs, hard-boiled and finely chopped
2 tablespoons cider vinegar or red wine vinegar
1 clove garlic, finely chopped
2 teaspoons finely chopped lemon balm
salt and freshly ground black pepper
8 lettuce leaves
4 twists of lemon
4 sprigs parsley

With a sharp knife, cut the avocados in half and remove the stones. Carefully scoop out the avocado flesh, leaving the skins intact, and transfer the flesh to a mixing bowl. Reserve the shells.

Using a fork, mash the avocado flesh with the eggs, vinegar, garlic, lemon balm, salt and pepper to a smooth paste. Spoon back into the skins and mark roughly with a fork.

Arrange the lettuce leaves on four individual serving dishes. Place a stuffed avocado half on top and garnish each portion with a twist of lemon and a sprig of parsley. Serve at once. *Serves 4*

Hummus

450 g (1 lb) cooked chick peas
2 tablespoons olive oil
1–2 cloves garlic, crushed
2 teaspoons lemon juice
½ teaspoon paprika
1 tablespoon sesame seeds (optional)
salt

Mash the chick peas well, using a fork. Add the oil, garlic and lemon juice and beat well. Add the paprika, seasame seeds and salt to taste. Alternatively, place all the ingredients in a liquidiser and purée at high speed until smooth.

Serve as a starter with raw vegetables such as strips of carrot or celery, cauliflower florets and spring onions. *Serves 4*

Stuffed Pears

225 g (8 oz) cream cheese
2 teaspoons finely chopped celery
few drops of Tabasco sauce
salt
50 g (2 oz) hazelnuts, finely chopped
4 ripe dessert pears
1 tablespoon lemon juice
few crisp lettuce leaves

Sieve the cream cheese into a small bowl. Add the celery and Tabasco and season to taste with salt. Form into small balls and roll in the finely chopped nuts.

Peel the pears, cut in half and remove the cores, using a teaspoon. Brush with lemon juice to prevent them from turning brown. Fill the pear cavities with the cheese balls and place on top of the lettuce leaves on four individual serving plates. *Serves 4*

Main Dishes

Soya Protein with Soured Cream

Cooking time 45 minutes

*175 g (6 oz) beef-flavoured soya protein
chunks*
*900 ml (1½ pints) dark vegetable stock
(see page 72)*
50 g (2 oz) butter
1 clove garlic, crushed
2 onions, peeled and finely chopped
*100 g (4 oz) mushrooms, wiped clean
and chopped*
salt and freshly ground black pepper
1 teaspoon freshly grated nutmeg
175 ml (6 fl oz) dry white wine
*2 teaspoons cornflour, mixed with
2 teaspoons dry white wine*
1 tablespoon made mustard
175 ml (6 fl oz) soured cream
1 tablespoon chopped parsley

Place the soya protein and the stock in a large bowl and
set aside to soak for 1 hour. Drain the chunks and discard
the stock.

In a large, flameproof casserole, melt the butter over a
moderate heat and add the garlic, onions and soya
chunks and cook, stirring constantly, for 3 minutes. Add
the mushrooms and continue cooking for 3–4 minutes,
or until the onions are soft but not brown.

Add the salt, pepper and nutmeg and stir in the wine
and cornflour. Increase the heat and bring the liquid to
the boil, stirring constantly. Reduce the heat and cook
for a further 20 minutes, stirring frequently.

In a small mixing bowl, combine the mustard and the
soured cream. Stir the mixture into the casserole and
continue cooking for 15 minutes.

Remove from the heat and sprinkle with the parsley.
Serve at once. *Serves 4*

77

Moussaka

Cooking time 35 minutes

*175 g (6 oz) textured vegetable protein
mince
900 ml (1½ pints) dark vegetable stock
(see page 72)
150 ml (¼ pint) oil
1 large onion, peeled and finely sliced
1 clove garlic, crushed
1 (396-g/14-oz) can tomatoes, drained
and chopped
65 g (2 oz) tomato purée
50 g (2 oz) mushrooms, wiped clean and
sliced
salt and freshly ground black pepper
¼ teaspoon cayenne pepper
2 large aubergines
25 g (1 oz) seasoned flour
350 ml (12 fl oz) hot béchamel sauce
(see page 109)
2 eggs, well beaten
50 g (2 oz) grated Parmesan cheese*

◆ ● ♥

Place the textured vegetable protein in a bowl and add the stock. Leave to soak for 6 minutes. Drain through a sieve and discard the stock.

In a large frying pan, heat 3 tablespoons of the oil, add the onion and garlic and cook, stirring occasionally, for 5–7 minutes or until the onion is soft and translucent but not brown. Stir in the mince, the tomatoes, tomato purée, mushrooms, salt, pepper and cayenne. Cook, stirring occasionally, for 5 minutes. Remove the pan from the heat.

Slice the aubergines and cover with salt, leave for 30 minutes then wash and dry well.

Coat the aubergine slices in the seasoned flour. In a second frying pan, heat half the remaining oil and add half the aubergine slices. Cook for 3 minutes on each side, until they are evenly browned. Set aside and cook the remaining aubergine slices in the same way, using the rest of the oil.

Arrange a third of the aubergine slices on the bottom of a 1·5-litre (2½-pint) ovenproof casserole. Top with half of the mince mixture. Continue making layers in this way, finishing with a layer of aubergine. Set aside.

In a medium bowl, combine the béchamel sauce, eggs,

and half the Parmesan cheese, beating until smooth.
Pour the mixture over the aubergine slices. Sprinkle
with the remaining Parmesan and bake in a moderate
oven (180°C, 350°F, Gas Mark 4) for 30–35 minutes, or
until the top is golden brown and bubbly. Serve at once
with a mixed salad. *Serves 4*

Bobotie

Cooking time 1 hour 20 minutes

1 tablespoon corn oil
225 g (8 oz) onions, peeled and sliced
675 g (1¼ lb) minced beef
1 small cooking apple, peeled and
chopped
1 tablespoon curry powder
50 g (2 oz) raisins
50 g (2 oz) peanuts
juice of 1 small lemon
salt and freshly ground black pepper
2 bay leaves
1 egg
150 ml (¼ pint) milk

◆ ● ♥

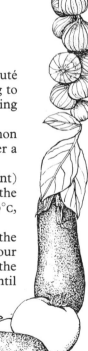

Heat the oil in a large saucepan and add the onion. Sauté
for 3 minutes, or until the onions are just beginning to
brown. Add the minced beef and apple. Sauté, stirring
constantly, for 3 minutes.

Add the curry powder, raisins, peanuts and lemon
juice with seasoning to taste. Mix well and cook over a
very low heat for 5 minutes.

Transfer the beef mixture to a 1-litre (1½-pint)
casserole. Press the bay leaves into the top of the
mixture, cover and bake in a moderate oven (180°C,
350°F, Gas Mark 4) for 45 minutes.

Meanwhile beat the egg with the milk. Remove the
cover from the casserole, discard the bay leaves and pour
the egg mixture over the meat. Return the dish to the
oven and bake, uncovered, for 15–20 minutes or until
the topping has set. *Serves 4*

Aubergine and Bean Casserole

Cooking time 3 hours plus 8 hours
soaking time

1 tablespoon oil
2 onions, peeled and sliced
4 carrots, scraped and sliced
2 sticks celery, scrubbed and chopped
1 kg (2 lb) middle neck of lamb, cubed
seasoned flour to coat
1 large aubergine, about 225 g (8 oz),
sliced
450 ml (¾ pint) dark vegetable stock
(see page 72)
100 g (4 oz) dried haricot beans, soaked
overnight
1 tablespoon tomato purée
salt and freshly ground black pepper

Heat the oil in a large frying pan and sauté the onions, carrots and celery for about 5 minutes. Remove from the pan, toss the trimmed lamb in the seasoned flour and fry until well browned. Return the vegetables to the pan and add the aubergine. Pour over the stock and add the remaining ingredients. Bring to the boil, cover and simmer for 2½ hours until the meat and beans are tender. Allow to cool (preferably overnight) then remove any surface fat before reheating for 15–20 minutes. Serve with a crisp salad and jacket potatoes. *Serves 4–6*

Honey-Glazed Chicken with Banana

Cooking time 45 minutes

1 (1·5-kg/3-lb) oven-ready chicken
1 tablespoon oil
4 tablespoons clear honey
½ teaspoon made mustard
3 teaspoons Worcestershire sauce
freshly ground black pepper
2 firm bananas, sliced

Cut the chicken in half through the breast bone. Lightly oil a roasting pan. Combine the honey, mustard, Worcestershire sauce and pepper. Place the chicken halves, skin side up in the pan, brush with the glaze and cook in a moderately hot oven (200°C, 400°F, Gas Mark 6) for 40 minutes. Brush with the glaze frequently.

When cooked, pour any juices from the chicken, free of excess fat, into a small saucepan. Add the bananas and heat through just enough to warm the banana. Spoon over the chicken and serve. *Serves 4*

Chicken Veronique with Yogurt

Cooking time 1 hour 10 minutes

4 chicken quarters
1½ teaspoons ground ginger
salt and freshly ground black pepper
225 g (8 oz) green grapes, halved and seeds removed
300 ml (½ pint) natural yogurt
1 tablespoon cornflour
50 g (2 oz) flaked almonds, toasted

◆ ○ ♡

Place the chicken quarters in an ovenproof casserole and sprinkle with the ground ginger and seasoning. Scatter the grapes over the chicken and add 300 ml (½ pint) water. Cover the casserole and bake in a moderate oven (180°C, 350°F, Gas Mark 4) for 1 hour or until the chicken is tender.

Transfer the chicken and grapes to a serving dish. Pour the yogurt into a mixing bowl and stir in the cornflour. Slowly pour the mixture from the casserole into the yogurt, whisking well. Return the mixture to the pan and cook over a low heat, stirring constantly, until the sauce is thickened. Season to taste and pour over the chicken and grapes. Sprinkle with the toasted almonds and serve immediately. *Serves 4*

Cassoulet

Cooking time 2¼ hours plus 12 hours
soaking time

225 g (8 oz) dried haricot beans
100 g (4 oz) streaky bacon
450 g (1 lb) belly of pork
225 g (8 oz) garlic sausage
4 small chicken quarters
900 ml (1½ pints) light vegetable stock
(see page 72)
225 g (8 oz) tomatoes, peeled and
chopped
1 bouquet garni
salt and freshly ground black pepper
100 g (4 oz) fresh breadcrumbs

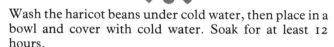

Wash the haricot beans under cold water, then place in a bowl and cover with cold water. Soak for at least 12 hours.

Chop the bacon and place in a large ovenproof casserole. Cut the belly of pork and garlic sausage into 2·5-cm (1-inch) cubes and add to the casserole with the chicken.

Drain the beans and add them to the casserole with the stock, tomatoes, bouquet garni and seasoning to taste. Mix well, cover and bake for 1½ hours.

Discard the bouquet garni and, if the mixture looks a little dry, add extra stock. Sprinkle with the bread crumbs and bake the casserole, uncovered, for an extra hour. This casserole improves on reheating. *Serves 4*

Grapefruit and Hazelnut Baked Trout

Cooking time 30 minutes

100 g (4 oz) shelled hazelnuts
4 medium trout, cleaned
salt and freshly ground black pepper
2 grapefruit

Place the hazelnuts under the grill and toast until brown. Remove and discard the thin brown skins.

Fill the cavities of the cleaned trout with the hazelnuts and place in a shallow, lightly oiled ovenproof dish. Season well with salt and pepper.

Cut the peel and pith from the grapefruit, working over the fish, so that any excess juice pours over them. Cut the membrane away from the fruit and place the segments around the fish.

Bake, uncovered, in a moderate oven (180°C, 350°F, Gas Mark 4) for 20–30 minutes, or until the trout are tender. *Serves 4*

Lentil Loaf

Cooking time 45–50 minutes

25 g (1 oz) butter or margarine
350 g (12 oz) lentils, cooked until tender
and drained
225 g (8 oz) Cheddar cheese, grated
2 medium onions, peeled and minced
50 g (2 oz) mushrooms, wiped clean and
thinly sliced
salt and freshly ground black pepper
¼ teaspoon ground cloves
1 tablespoon finely chopped parsley
75 g (3 oz) stale brown breadcrumbs
1 egg, lightly beaten
3 tablespoons double cream
few sprigs parsley

◆ ● ♥

Grease a 0·5-kg (1-lb) loaf tin with 1 tablespoon of the butter and set aside.

In a large mixing bowl, combine the lentils, cheese, onions, mushrooms, salt, pepper, cloves and parsley. Mix well. Add the breadcrumbs, egg and cream and beat until the ingredients are well mixed.

Pour the mixture into the loaf tin. Cut the remaining butter or margarine into small pieces and dot them over the top of the loaf. Bake in a moderate oven (180°C, 350°F, Gas Mark 4) for 45–50 minutes, or until the loaf is firm and a skewer inserted into the centre comes out clean.

Turn on to a warmed serving dish, garnish with parsley and serve hot with a spicy tomato sauce. *Serves 6*

Bean and Fruit Stew

Cooking time 1¼ hours

225 g (8 oz) dried haricot beans,
soaked overnight
1·75 litres (3 pints) dark vegetable stock
(see page 72)
450 g (1 lb) French beans, washed and
trimmed
450 g (1 lb) carrots, scraped and sliced
2 medium potatoes, scrubbed and
quartered
75 g (3 oz) butter or margarine
2 medium onions, peeled and sliced
250 ml (8 fl oz) dry cider
½ teaspoon black pepper
¼ teaspoon grated nutmeg
½ teaspoon dried marjoram
¼ teaspoon dried basil
450 g (1 lb) cooking apples, peeled,
cored and cut into large cubes
1 banana, sliced
50 g (2 oz) fresh or canned and drained
pineapple, chopped
1 (213-g/7½-oz) can prunes, drained
and stoned

◇ ◑ ♥

Drain the beans and put into a large saucepan. Pour over half the stock and bring to the boil. Reduce the heat and simmer for 45 minutes, or until just tender.

Add the French beans, carrots and potatoes to the beans. Pour over the remaining stock. Increase the heat and bring back to the boil. Reduce the heat and cook for 15–20 minutes, or until tender, stirring occasionally.

Meanwhile, in a small saucepan, melt the fat and add the onions. Sauté, stirring occasionally, for 5–7 minutes, until they are soft and translucent but not brown. Add the onions to the beans and vegetables, stir in and continue cooking for a further 5 minutes. Pour in the cider and add the pepper, nutmeg, marjoram and basil. Taste and add salt if necessary. Bring to the boil. Reduce the heat and stir in the apples. Cover and simmer, stirring occasionally, for about 10 minutes.

Stir in the banana, pineapple and prunes and continue simmering the stew for 5 minutes.

Serve at once, or leave until cold and serve slightly chilled. Serve with crusty bread and cider as a light main dish. *Serves 6*

Aubergine and bean casserole (see page 80)

Butter Bean and Tomato Pie

Cooking time 35 minutes

Filling
50 g (2 oz) butter
1 large onion, peeled and chopped
½ teaspoon dried basil
1 (425-g/15-oz) can butter beans
1 tablespoon tomato chutney
1 (425-g/15-oz) can tomatoes
1 teaspoon lemon juice
salt and freshly ground black pepper

Pastry
175 g (6 oz) plain wholemeal flour
½ teaspoon salt
75 g (3 oz) butter
4 tablespoons cold water

◆ ● ♥

Melt the butter in a frying pan. Add the onion and cook, stirring occasionally, for about 10 minutes. Remove from the heat and add the basil, drained butter beans, chutney, tomatoes (with can juice), lemon juice and seasoning to taste. Put into a 20-cm (8-inch) pie dish and leave to cool.

Sift the flour and salt into a large mixing bowl, add any residue of bran left in the sieve. Rub in the butter until the mixture resembles fine breadcrumbs, then add the cold water to make a dough. Roll out on a floured surface to fit the pie dish. Line the dish rim with a strip of pastry before placing the pie lid on top. Seal the edges and flute. Make a hole in the centre for the steam to escape, then decorate with any remaining pastry trimmings.

Bake in a moderately hot oven (200°C, 400°F, Gas Mark 6) for 30 minutes until the pastry is crisp and the filling is heated through. *Serves 4*

87

Butter bean and tomato pie (see above) ; Courgette refresher salad (see page 100)

Wholemeal Pizza with Green Pepper and Mushrooms

Cooking time 15 minutes plus 1½ hours rising time

Base
2 teaspoons dried yeast
1 teaspoon sugar
150 ml (¼ pint) lukewarm water
225 g (8 oz) plain wholemeal flour
pinch of salt
¼ teaspoon olive oil

Topping
1 (396-g/14-oz) can tomatoes
1 onion, peeled and chopped
2 cloves garlic, crushed
salt and freshly ground black pepper
225 g (8 oz) Mozzarella cheese, sliced
2 teaspoons dried marjoram or oregano
1 green pepper, seeds removed, cut into rings
100 g (4 oz) button mushrooms, wiped clean and cut into thin slices
4 tablespoons olive oil

Stir the yeast and the sugar into half the water. Leave in a warm place until frothy – about 10–15 minutes.

Put the flour and the salt into a bowl and add the yeast mixture, the remaining water and olive oil. Turn on to a lightly floured board and knead for 5–10 minutes, until smooth and elastic. Return to the bowl and cover with cling film or a cloth. Stand in a warm place until the dough has doubled in size – about 1½ hours.

Meanwhile, empty the contents of the can of tomatoes into a saucepan with the onion and garlic and simmer, uncovered, for about 30 minutes, until reduced to a thick purée. Season to taste.

Divide the yeast dough into four pieces and roll each piece into a circle about 15 cm (6 inches) in diameter. Place the circles on two well oiled baking sheets. Cover with the tomato sauce, sprinkle with cheese and herbs, then arrange the green pepper rings and sliced mushrooms attractively on top of the pizzas.

Cook in a moderately hot oven (200°C, 400°C, Gas Mark 6) for about 15 minutes. Serve at once. *Serves 4*

Cheese and Eggs

Home-Made Cottage Cheese

*Cooking time 15 minutes plus 24 hours
draining time*

600 ml (1 pint) milk
1½ teaspoons rennet
salt and freshly ground white pepper

Heat the milk in a saucepan until just tepid. Mix in the rennet. Pour into a bowl and leave in a warm place for 15 minutes, or until the milk has set and curds have formed.

Stand over a saucepan of hot water. Gently heat to 43°C (110°F), just hand hot. Cook until the curds and whey separate – about 6–8 hours. Line a sieve with muslin and strain the mixture over a bowl. Tie the corners of the muslin together to form a bag and suspend the bag over the bowl for 12–24 hours to remove all the whey.

Mash the drained curds with a fork and season to taste with salt and pepper. Store, covered, in the refrigerator for up to a week. *Makes 100 g (4 oz)*

Cheese Loaf

350 g (12 oz) cheese, grated
100 g (4 oz) walnuts, chopped
salt and freshly ground black pepper
pinch of dry mustard
225 g (8 oz) cottage cheese
6 tablespoons mayonnaise (see page 110)
15 g (½ oz) gelatine, dissolved in 3 tablespoons hot water

Mix the cheese, walnuts, seasoning and mustard together in a mixing bowl, then fold in the cottage cheese and mayonnaise with the dissolved gelatine. Pour into a greased 0·5-kg (1-lb) loaf tin and chill until set in the refrigerator. Turn out on to a serving dish and garnish with salad vegetables. *Serves 6*

89

Cheese Charlotte

Cooking time 40 minutes

1 teaspoon vegetable oil
1 thick slice bread, cut into cubes
200 ml (7 fl oz) milk
8 slices of bread, crusts removed
40 g (1½ oz) butter or margarine
3 eggs, separated
1½ tablespoons flour
225 g (8 oz) Cheddar cheese, grated
¼ teaspoon salt
¼ teaspoon grated nutmeg
6 tablespoons single cream

Lightly grease a deep, 23-cm (9-inch) straight-sided dish or casserole with the oil and set aside.

Put the bread cubes in a bowl and sprinkle with half the milk. In another bowl, spread out the bread slices and soak them in the remaining milk.

Cream the fat until soft. Mix in the egg yolks, one at a time. Stir in the flour and add the bread cubes, cheese, salt and nutmeg. Mix well and stir in the cream.

Beat the egg whites until stiff and fold into the cheese mixture.

Line the dish with the soaked bread slices and pour in the cheese mixture. Bake in a moderate oven (180°C, 350°F, Gas Mark 4) for 35–40 minutes, or until the charlotte is puffed up and lightly browned. Serve with a crunchy salad and onion and herb loaf (see page 120). *Serves 4*

Mediterranean Omelette

Cooking time 10 minutes

15 g (½ oz) butter
1 small onion, peeled and finely chopped
1 clove garlic, crushed
100 g (4 oz) mushrooms, wiped clean
and sliced
2 tomatoes, peeled and sliced
2 eggs
150 ml/¼ pint milk
salt and freshly ground black pepper
watercress

Melt the butter in an omelette or frying pan and sauté the onion until cooked but not coloured. Add the garlic and mushrooms and cook for 2–3 minutes. Add the tomatoes and cook for 1 minute.

Beat the eggs, milk and seasoning together, pour over the vegetable mixture and cook over a low heat until set. Serve cut in wedges, garnished with watercress. *Serves 2*

Spiced Egg Ragoût

Cooking time 40 minutes

225 g (8 oz) baby onions
450 g (1 lb) medium potatoes
50 g (2 oz) butter or margarine
1 teaspoon chilli seasoning
1 teaspoon ground cardamom
½ teaspoon ground coriander
½ teaspoon ground turmeric
2 tablespoons flour
1 (396-g/14-oz) can tomatoes
1 clove garlic, crushed
300 ml (½ pint) light vegetable stock
(see page 72)
1 (142-ml/5-fl oz) carton natural
yogurt
salt and freshly ground black pepper
8 eggs, hard-boiled
chopped parsley

Peel and halve the onions, peel the potatoes and cut into finger size pieces. Lightly brown the onions and potatoes in the hot fat in a large saucepan. Add the chilli seasoning, cardamom, coriander, turmeric and flour and cook for 1 minute, stirring all the time.

Add the tomatoes with the juice from the can, the garlic, stock, yogurt and seasoning to taste. Bring to the boil, then cover and simmer gently for about 40 minutes.

Shell the eggs and cut in half lengthwise. Add to the sauce and leave over a low heat to warm through. Sprinkle with chopped parsley before serving. *Serves 4*

Vegetables

Caponata

Cooking time 40 minutes

4 small aubergines
2 teaspoons salt
6 tablespoons oil
4 sticks celery, cleaned and finely
chopped
2 large onions, peeled and thinly sliced
6 tablespoons tomato purée, diluted with
3 tablespoons water
1 tablespoon capers
50 g (2 oz) green olives, stoned and
chopped
4½ tablespoons red wine vinegar
1 tablespoon sugar

◇ ◑ ♡

Peel and dice the aubergines. Place in a colander and sprinkle with salt. Leave for 30 minutes. Rinse under cold water and pat dry using kitchen paper.

In a large frying pan, heat 4½ tablespoons of the oil. Add the diced aubergines and cook for 8–10 minutes, or until the pieces are soft and brown. Drain on kitchen paper and set aside.

Pour the remaining oil into the frying pan and add the celery and onions. Cook for 8–10 minutes, or until they are lightly coloured. Pour in the tomato purée mixture and stir to coat the vegetables. Reduce the heat, cover the pan and simmer for 15 minutes.

Stir in the capers, olives, vinegar and sugar, and mix until all the ingredients are combined. Return the aubergine pieces to the pan and coat them thoroughly with the sauce. Reduce the heat and cook the mixture for 20 minutes.

Turn the caponata into a serving dish. Allow to cool to room temperature then refrigerate. Chill for at least 2 hours before serving. Serve as a starter or special accompaniment to a main meal. *Serves 4–6*

Vegetable Crêpes

*Cooking time 10 minutes plus few
minutes for each crêpe*

Crêpe Batter
*225 g (8 oz) flour
½ teaspoon salt
4 eggs
4 tablespoons melted butter
250 ml (8 fl oz) milk
250 ml (8 fl oz) water
2 tablespoons oil*

Filling
*3 tablespoons oil
2 onions, peeled and finely chopped
1 small red pepper, seeds removed and
chopped
½ small green cabbage, shredded
1 small apple, peeled, cored and chopped
salt and freshly ground black pepper
1 teaspoon dried dill leaves*

Make the batter by sifting the flour and salt into a mixing bowl. Make a well in the centre and add the eggs and the melted butter. With a wooden spoon, gently fold in the flour. Gradually add the milk and water until the mixture forms a smooth batter. Leave in a cool place for about 2 hours.

With a pastry brush, lightly grease a heavy medium frying pan with a little of the oil. Place the pan over a moderate heat and warm the oil until it is very hot. Remove the pan from the heat and pour about 4 tablespoons of the batter into the centre of the pan. Quickly tilt the pan in all directions. Return the pan to the heat and cook for just over 1 minute. Shake the pan to loosen the crêpe. Turn the crêpe over and cook for 30 seconds. Remove and keep warm.

In a medium frying pan, heat the oil for the vegetable mixture. When hot, add the onion and red pepper and cook for 5 minutes. Add the cabbage, apple, salt, pepper and dill to the pan and cook for a further 5 minutes. Remove from the heat.

Place 1–2 tablespoons of the mixture on the centre of each crêpe and roll up around the filling. Serve at once.
Serves 4

Stuffed Leeks Olympia

Cooking time 30 minutes

450 g (1 lb) leeks
2 tablespoons fresh wholemeal
breadcrumbs
½ teaspoon dried thyme
25 g (1 oz) cheese, grated
½ egg yolk
salt and freshly ground black pepper
450 ml (¾ pint) béchamel sauce
(see page 109)
¼ teaspoon curry powder
1 (142-ml / 5-fl oz) carton natural
yogurt
grilled mushrooms
chopped parsley

◈ ◑ ♥

Cut and trim the leeks into 10-cm (4-inch) lengths. Wash and cook in boiling, salted water for 2 minutes.

Meanwhile, bind the breadcrumbs, thyme and cheese with the egg yolk. Split the leeks in half, almost to the base, and fill with the stuffing. Place in a shallow casserole dish, cover and bake in a moderately hot oven (190°C, 375°F, Gas Mark 5) for 30 minutes.

Place the sauce in a bowl, add the curry powder and the yogurt. Pour over the leeks and garnish with the grilled mushrooms and chopped parsley. *Serves 4*

Green Peppers with Brown Rice and Walnut Stuffing

Cooking time 1½ hours

4 green peppers, seeds removed
2 tablespoons oil
1 onion, peeled and chopped
1 large clove garlic, crushed
50 g (2 oz) brown rice
1 bay leaf
450 ml (¾ pint) tomato juice
1 teaspoon dried basil
100 g (4 oz) walnuts, chopped
salt and freshly ground black pepper
50 g (2 oz) cheese, grated

◈ ● ♥

Cut a small slice off the top of each green pepper and reserve. Core, rinse and dry the peppers.

Heat the oil in a saucepan, add the onion and garlic and cook, stirring occasionally, for about 10 minutes. Add the rice, bay leaf and half the tomato juice. Cover and simmer for 40 minutes, or until the rice is tender.

Remove the bay leaf. Add the basil, walnuts and seasoning to the mixture.

Fill the peppers with the rice mixture, place in a greased casserole and sprinkle with the grated cheese. Replace the sliced-off tops of the peppers to form lids. Pour the remaining tomato juice around the peppers. Bake in a moderate oven (180°C, 350°F, Gas Mark 4) for 30–40 minutes until cooked. *Serves 4*

Stuffed Mushrooms

Cooking time 20 minutes

12 large, flat mushrooms
salt and freshly ground black pepper
1 teaspoon melted butter
25 g (1 oz) butter
2 shallots or spring onions, peeled and
finely chopped
1 tablespoon flour
6 tablespoons single cream
3 tablespoons finely chopped parsley
1½ tablespoons grated Parmesan cheese

Remove the stalks from the mushrooms and set aside. Season the mushroom caps with salt and pepper and coat with the melted butter. Arrange them, hollow sides up, in a lightly greased shallow baking dish.

Finely chop the mushroom stalks. Wrap them in kitchen paper and twist to extract the juice. Fry the stalks in the butter with the shallots or spring onions for 3–4 minutes. Reduce the heat and stir in the flour. Cook for 1 minute. Stir in the cream away from the heat. When smooth, simmer for 2–3 minutes until thick. Stir in the parsley and season to taste.

Divide the mixture between the prepared mushroom caps. Top each with a little grated cheese. Bake in a moderately hot oven (190°C, 375°F, Gas Mark 5) for 15 minutes, or until tender. *Serves 4*

Minted Tomato Ratatouille

Cooking time 20 minutes

450 g (1 lb) tomatoes
225 g (8 oz) courgettes
225 g (8 oz) onions
100 g (4 oz) button mushrooms
1 green pepper, seeds removed
4 tablespoons oil
2 tablespoons chopped mint
salt and freshly ground black pepper
grated Parmesan cheese

Peel and quarter the tomatoes, and remove the seeds, reserving the juices. Wipe the courgettes and cut into 5-mm ($\frac{1}{4}$-inch) slices. Peel and slice the onions. Wipe the mushrooms and slice thickly. Slice the pepper thinly.

Heat the oil in a large saucepan and fry the courgettes and onions together until golden, stirring occasionally. Add half the tomatoes and their juices, the mushrooms, pepper, mint and seasoning to taste. Cover and simmer gently for 15 minutes.

Stir in the remaining tomatoes and reheat gently for about 5 minutes. Serve hot or cold, dusted with Parmesan cheese. *Serves 4*

Brompton Brussels

Cooking time 20 minutes

450 g (1 lb) potatoes
450 g (1 lb) baby Brussels sprouts
freshly ground black pepper
300 ml ($\frac{1}{2}$ pint) natural yogurt
25 g (1 oz) red cheese, grated

Scrub the potatoes and cook in boiling, salted water for about 20 minutes, or until tender. Drain, cool and dice.

Trim the sprouts and cook in boiling, salted water for about 6–8 minutes, or until tender. Slice and place in a bowl with the diced potato. Season with black pepper and carefully fold in the yogurt. Chill.

To serve, place the mixture in a salad bowl. Sprinkle with the grated cheese and serve as a side salad or as a vegetable with hot or cold savoury dishes. *Serves 6*

Salads

Pecan Peach Salad

4 ripe peaches, peeled, halved and stoned
2 tablespoons lemon juice
225 g (8 oz) cottage cheese
100 g (4 oz) pecan nuts, finely chopped
8 lettuce leaves

Place the peaches in a mixing bowl and sprinkle with the lemon juice. Toss until well coated in juice.

Mix together the cottage cheese and pecan nuts. Arrange the lettuce leaves on four individual serving dishes. Place two peach halves on each dish, cut sides up. Spoon the cottage cheese mixture into the centres and serve. *Serves 4*

Cracked Wheat Salad

100 g (4 oz) cracked wheat
2 tablespoons finely chopped shallots or
spring onions
6 tablespoons chopped parsley
6 tablespoons chopped mint
2 tablespoons olive oil
2 tablespoons lemon juice
salt and freshly ground black pepper
black olives
2 tomatoes, sliced

Place the cracked wheat in a bowl and cover with cold water. Leave to soak for 30 minutes. Drain, then wrap in a tea towel and squeeze to extract as much moisture as possible.

Put in a bowl and add the shallots or spring onions, parsley, mint, oil and lemon juice. Season to taste with salt and pepper. Place the mixture in a shallow serving dish and garnish with black olives and sliced tomatoes. *Serves 4*

Bean Sprout Salad

225 g (8 oz) fresh or canned bean
sprouts, drained
1 canned pimiento, drained and chopped
1 pickled cucumber, diced
1 tablespoon finely chopped chives

Dressing
2 tablespoons olive oil
1 tablespoon wine vinegar
¼ teaspoon made mustard
2 teaspoons soy sauce
¼ teaspoon sugar
¼ teaspoon salt

Put the bean sprouts in a salad bowl with the pimiento, pickled cucumber and chives.

Mix together all the ingredients for the dressing, making sure that the sugar is completely dissolved. Pour the dressing over the salad and toss to coat thoroughly. Chill for about 30 minutes before serving. *Serves 4*

Napoleon's Bean Salad
Cooking time 3 hours

225 g (8 oz) dried haricot beans, soaked
overnight
1 onion, peeled and quartered
1 carrot, scraped and quartered
1 bouquet garni
salt and freshly ground black pepper
4 tablespoons finely chopped herbs or
spring onion
5 tablespoons olive oil
1 tablespoon tarragon vinegar
1 teaspoon French mustard
¼ teaspoon castor sugar

Drain the beans and put in a large pan or casserole. Add the onion and carrot quarters, bouquet garni and a generous sprinkling of black pepper. Pour over sufficient water to cover. Simmer gently over a low heat for 2–3 hours. Replenish the water from time to time so that the beans do not dry out.

Season the booked beans to taste with salt and cook for

a further 5 minutes. Drain and discard the vegetables and bouquet garni. Stir the beans, herbs, oil, vinegar, mustard and sugar together in a bowl. Chill for 1 hour. *Serves 6*

Mixed Bean Salad

Cooking time 1 hour

275 g (10 oz) mixed dried beans, such as
aduki, red kidney, haricot etc.
6 tablespoons French dressing
½ teaspoon ground coriander
50 g (2 oz) onion, peeled and cut in rings
salt and freshly ground black pepper

Soak the beans overnight. Drain and cook in boiling salted water until tender – about 1 hour. Drain and place in a large mixing bowl.

While the beans are still warm, pour over the French dressing with the coriander. Toss well and cool.

Toss the onion with the beans, season to taste and chill before serving. *Serves 6*

Bean and Cauliflower Salad

Cooking time 1–2 hours

250 g (9 oz) dried red kidney beans
2 medium cauliflowers, trimmed
175 g (6 oz) leeks
2 tablespoons tarragon vinegar
6 tablespoons oil
salt and freshly ground black pepper

Soak the kidney beans in cold water overnight. Drain, place in fresh water and simmer, covered, for 1½–2 hours or until tender.

Trim the cauliflower and break into florets. Blanch in boiling, salted water for 3 minutes and cool under cold running water.

Halve the leeks down the centre and slice finely. Wash well. Place in a screw-topped jar with the vinegar, oil and seasoning and shake well.

Pour the dressing over the warm beans and cauliflower. Cover and chill before serving. *Serves 8*

Courgette Refresher Salad

Cooking time 8 minutes plus 2 hours
marinating time

8 courgettes
1 medium Spanish onion, peeled and
finely chopped
1 clove garlic, finely chopped
4–6 tablespoons French dressing
lettuce leaves
4 tomatoes, peeled and finely chopped
½ small green pepper, seeds removed and
finely chopped
1 tablespoon capers, finely chopped
¼ teaspoon chopped basil
¼ teaspoon chopped parsley
salt and freshly ground black pepper

◇ ○ ♡

Simmer the courgettes, unpeeled, in salted water for about 8 minutes. Cut in half lengthwise and carefully scoop out the seeds. Lay the courgettes, cut sides up, in a flat dish.

Combine half the finely chopped onion with the garlic and cover the courgettes with this mixture. Sprinkle half the French dressing over them, cover and allow to marinate in the refrigerator for at least 2 hours.

To serve, remove the onion and garlic mixture and drain off the marinade. Arrange the courgettes on crisp lettuce leaves and fill the hollows with the remaining French dressing, to which you have added the remaining onion, the finely chopped tomatoes, green pepper, capers, basil and parsley. Season to taste before serving.
Serves 4

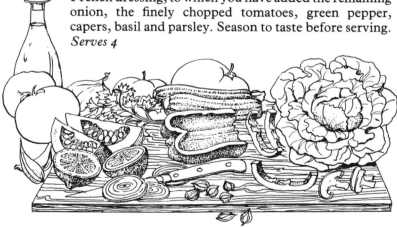

Cereals, Pasta and Nuts

Vegetable Rice with Roasted Cashew Nuts

Cooking time 45 minutes

175 g (6 oz) cashew nuts
3–4 tablespoons oil
salt
50 g (2 oz) butter
1 medium onion, peeled and chopped
1 clove garlic, crushed
225 g (8 oz) brown long-grain rice
450 ml (¾ pint) water
¼ teaspoon ground turmeric
1 teaspoon sea salt
1 large carrot, scraped and diced
225 g (8 oz) French beans, cut into 5-cm (2-inch) pieces
1 small red pepper, seeds removed and chopped
4 tomatoes, peeled and quartered
freshly ground black pepper

◊ ◖ ♥

First prepare the cashew nuts by frying gently in the oil, turning constantly until golden brown. Drain on absorbent paper and sprinkle with a little salt.

Melt the butter in a saucepan. Add the onion and garlic and cook gently, stirring occasionally, until they are soft and translucent but not coloured. Add the rice, water, turmeric and sea salt and bring to the boil. Cover and simmer very gently for 40 minutes, until the rice is tender.

Meanwhile, cook the carrot, beans and pepper in boiling salted water until tender. Using a fork, carefully mix the cooked vegetables and tomatoes into the rice, together with half the roasted cashew nuts. Check the seasoning and adjust if necessary.

Serve in a large shallow dish, sprinkled with the remaining cashew nuts. *Serves 4*

Sesame Seed and Honey Fingers

Cooking time 5–6 minutes

75 g (3 oz) butter
1 tablespoon sesame seeds
1 tablespoon thick honey
8 thin slices bread, toasted on one side
and with crusts removed

In a small mixing bowl, cream the butter with a wooden spoon until soft and fluffy. Beat in the sesame seeds and honey.

Place the toast slices, untoasted side up, on the grill rack. Spread each slice liberally with the sesame seed mixture. Cook under a hot grill for 5–6 minutes or until the tops are brown and bubbling.

Remove from the heat and cut each side into three fingers. Serve at once as an accompaniment to soups. *Serves 4*

Pine Kernel Dumplings

Cooking time 15 minutes

75 g (3 oz) flour
salt and freshly ground black pepper
50 g (2 oz) butter or margarine
3 tablespoons ground pine kernels
75 g (3 oz) fresh brown breadcrumbs
1 teaspoon dried basil
1 egg, lightly beaten
3 tablespoons water

Sift the flour, salt and pepper into a mixing bowl. Add the butter or margarine and rub in with the fingertips, until the mixture resembles coarse breadcrumbs.

Stir in the pine kernels, breadcrumbs and basil. Make a well in the centre of the flour mixture and pour in the egg and half the water. Gradually draw the flour mixture into the water and egg, until all the flour has been incorporated. Add more water if the dough is too dry.

Form the mixture into small balls and drop them into boiling soups, stews or casseroles. Simmer for 15 minutes. Serve at once. *Makes 12*

Yogurt and orange whip (see page 116) ; Cider fruit salad (see page 115)

Rice and Pistachio Nut Ring

Cooking time 20 minutes

50 g (2 oz) blanched almonds
25 g (1 oz) walnuts
15 g ($\frac{1}{2}$ oz) pistachio nuts, peeled and
split
25 g (1 oz) butter or margarine
1 tablespoon corn oil
225 g (8 oz) cold cooked rice

Coarsely chop the almonds, walnuts and pistachios. Heat the fat and corn oil in a saucepan and add the nuts. Cook, stirring constantly, for about 30 seconds, or until the nuts are golden brown. Spoon the nuts into a lightly greased 1-litre (1½-pint) ring mould.

Press the cold cooked rice on top of the nuts, cover with foil and bake in a moderate oven (180°C, 350°F, Gas Mark 4) for 15 minutes. Invert on to a plate and serve at once. *Serves 4*

Spiced Nuts

Cooking time few minutes

225 g (8 oz) light raw cane sugar
1 teaspoon ground cinnamon
finely grated rind of 1 orange
pinch of mace
6 tablespoons milk
1 teaspoon butter
1 teaspoon vanilla essence
275 g (10 oz) walnut halves

Combine the sugar, cinnamon, orange rind, mace and milk. Cook until the mixture reaches the soft ball stage – 113°C/236°F on a sugar thermometer. Remove from the heat and add the butter. Leave to stand for a few minutes, then add the vanilla and nuts.

Stir quickly until thick, then turn out on to waxed paper. Quickly separate the nuts, using a skewer, and allow to dry. Serve as nibbles.

Sunflower seed walnut bars (see page 126); Farmhouse orchard scones (see page 125); Natural health candy (see page 126); Onion and herb loaf (see page 120)

Barley and Mushroom Pilaf

Cooking time 1 hour

2 tablespoons corn oil
1 large onion, peeled and finely chopped
100 g (4 oz) mushrooms, wiped clean
and sliced
175 g (6 oz) pearl barley
450 ml (¾ pint) light vegetable stock
(see page 72)
salt and freshly ground black pepper
1 bay leaf
25 g (1 oz) Cheddar cheese, grated

◊ ◑ ♡

Heat the oil in a frying pan and add the chopped onion. Cook, stirring frequently, for 3 minutes. Add the mushrooms and cook for 1 minute. Add the pearl barley and cook for 1 minute more, stirring occasionally.

Transfer to an oven-proof dish and pour in the stock. Season to taste and add the bay leaf. Cover the dish and refrigerate for at least 2 hours or preferably overnight.

Bake the casserole, covered, in a moderately hot oven (190°C, 375°F, Gas Mark 5) for 1 hour, or until all the stock is absorbed and the barley is tender but still slightly chewy.

Serve at once, topped with the grated cheese. *Serves 4*

Oriental Pasta Salad

Cooking time 12–15 minutes

175 g (6 oz) pasta shapes
2 carrots, scraped and grated
1 (200-g/7-oz) can pineapple chunks
175 g (6 oz) fresh bean sprouts
25 g (1 oz) sprouted fenugreek
½ small cucumber, finely sliced

Dressing
2 tablespoons pineapple juice
1 tablespoon soy sauce
2 tablespoons orange juice
6 tablespoons oil

Cook the pasta shapes in boiling, salted water for about 12–15 minutes, or until just tender. Mix with the carrots, diced pineapple chunks to taste, bean sprouts, fenugreek and cucumber.

Make the dressing by placing all the ingredients in a small bowl and beating vigorously with a fork. Add the dressing to the pasta and toss to coat. Allow to cool before serving. *Serves 4*

Note This dish can be prepared using wholemeal pasta as an interesting variation.

Wheatgerm Stuffing

4 tablespoons wheatgerm
2 tablespoons chopped parsley
1 large flat mushroom, wiped clean and chopped
1 small onion, peeled and finely chopped
1 tablespoon oil or melted butter
1 egg yolk
1 teaspoon lemon juice
1 teaspoon dried thyme or 2 teaspoons fresh thyme, chopped
pinch of marjoram
pinch of freshly grated nutmeg
salt and freshly ground black pepper
water, dry red or white wine to mix

◈ ◑ ◗

Mix together the wheatgerm, parsley, mushroom, onion, oil, egg yolk and the lemon juice. Add the thyme, marjoram, nutmeg and seasoning and add water or wine to bind.

Use to stuff potatoes or a small chicken or for making beef olives.

Sauces and Dressings

White Sauce

Cooking time 5 minutes

25 g (1 oz) butter
2 tablespoons flour
600 ml (1 pint) milk
salt and freshly ground white pepper

In a medium saucepan, melt the butter over a low heat. Remove from the heat, add the flour and mix to a smooth paste. Gradually add the milk, stirring constantly.

Bring to the boil, reduce the heat and simmer for 2–3 minutes, until the sauce is thick and smooth. Season and use as required. *Makes 600 ml (1 pint)*

Variations

Mustard sauce Add 2 teaspoons French mustard to the above recipe.

Caper sauce Add 2 tablespoons capers and 2 tablespoons chopped parsley to the above recipe.

Egg sauce Add 4 chopped hard-boiled eggs to the above recipe.

Cheese sauce Add 50 g (2 oz) grated cheese, 50 g (2 oz) grated Parmesan cheese and 1 teaspoon French mustard to the above recipe.

Brown Sauce

Cooking time 10 minutes

25 g (1 oz) butter
2 tablespoons flour
600 ml (1 pint) dark vegetable stock
(see page 72)
1 tablespoon yeast extract

In a medium saucepan, melt the butter over a moderate heat. Add the flour and mix to a smooth paste. Cook for about 4 minutes, or until the roux turns dark brown.

Remove from the heat and gradually add the stock, stirring constantly. Return to the heat and bring the sauce to the boil. Reduce the heat, add the yeast extract and simmer for about 3 minutes, until the sauce is thick and smooth. Use as required. This sauce is delicious with a nut roast or savoury quiche. *Makes 600 ml (1 pint)*

Béchamel Sauce

Cooking time 10 minutes

600 ml (1 pint) milk
1 bay leaf
1 blade of mace
1 onion, peeled and halved
6 black peppercorns
¼ teaspoon salt
25 g (1 oz) butter
2 tablespoons flour

Pour the milk into a medium saucepan. Add the bay leaf, mace, onion, peppercorns and salt. Warm the milk gently for about 7 minutes to infuse the flavour.

Remove the pan from the heat and strain the milk into a small bowl. Discard the seasonings and onion.

Melt the butter in a small saucepan. Stir in the flour to make a smooth paste. Gradually add the milk, then bring to the boil. Simmer for about 2–3 minutes until smooth and thick. Use as required. *Makes 600 ml (1 pint)*

Horseradish and Soured Cream Dressing

4 tablespoons freshly grated horseradish
1 tablespoon vinegar
1 (142-ml/5-fl oz) carton soured cream
1 teaspoon sugar
¼ teaspoon salt
¼ teaspoon cayenne pepper

Using a wooden spoon, combine the horseradish, vinegar, soured cream, sugar, salt and cayenne.

Carefully spoon the sauce into a sauceboat and chill in the refrigerator until required. Serve with any cold vegetable or salad dish. *Makes 250 ml (8 fl oz)*

Lemon Sauce

Cooking time 15 minutes

300 ml (½ pint) light vegetable stock
(see page 72)
2 tablespoons cornflour, mixed with
3 tablespoons water
2 egg yolks
2 tablespoons lemon juice
2 teaspoons grated lemon rind
1 tablespoon butter, cut into small pieces

In a medium sized saucepan, bring the stock to the boil over a moderate heat. Reduce to a simmer and add the cornflour and water. Simmer for 8 minutes, stirring.

In a small bowl, beat the egg yolks and the lemon juice together. Stir in 2 tablespoons of the hot stock mixture. Add the egg yolk mixture to the remaining stock in the saucepan with the lemon rind. Simmer for 5 minutes.

Add the butter, one piece at a time, still stirring. When all the butter has melted in, serve the sauce with green vegetables. *Makes 600 ml (1 pint)*

Mayonnaise

2 egg yolks, at room temperature
salt and freshly ground black pepper
¾ teaspoon dry mustard
250 ml (8 fl oz) olive oil, at room
temperature
1 tablespoon white wine vinegar or lemon
juice

Place the egg yolks, salt, pepper and mustard in a medium mixing bowl and, using a wire whisk, beat the ingredients together until they are thoroughly blended. Add the oil, a few drops at a time, whisking constantly. Do not add the oil too quickly or the mayonnaise will curdle. After the mayonnaise has thickened, the oil may be added a little more rapidly.

Beat in a few drops of lemon juice or vinegar from time to time to prevent the mayonnaise from becoming too thick. When all the oil has been added, stir in the remaining lemon juice or vinegar, and season to taste. *Makes 300 ml (½ pint)*

Yogurt Dressing

250 ml (8 fl oz) mayonnaise
(see page 110)
4 tablespoons natural yogurt
1 teaspoon sugar
¼ teaspoon salt
1 tablespoon grated onion
1 tablespoon finely chopped celery

Mix the mayonnaise with the yogurt in a medium mixing bowl until well combined. Add the remaining ingredients and beat for 1 minute. Use at once. *Makes 350 ml (12 fl oz)*

Honey Dressing

2 tablespoons clear honey
4 tablespoons lemon juice
6 tablespoons olive oil
¼ teaspoon French mustard
salt and freshly ground black pepper

In a small mixing bowl, beat all the ingredients together, using a fork, until they are well combined.

Alternatively place all the ingredients together in a screw-topped jar and shake for 10 seconds. Use as required. *Makes 175 ml (6 fl oz)*
Note Corn oil reduces this to a low cholesterol recipe.

French Dressing

2 tablespoons red wine vinegar
4½ tablespoons olive oil
salt and freshly ground black pepper

In a small mixing bowl, beat all the ingredients together until they are well combined.

Alternatively, put all the ingredients in a screw-topped jar and shake for about 10 seconds. Use the dressing as required. *Makes 100 ml (4 fl oz)*
Note Corn oil reduces this to a low cholesterol recipe.

Desserts

Oaten Honeycomb

Cooking time 1¼ hours

450 ml (¾ pint) milk
175 g (6 oz) rolled oats
50 g (2 oz) raw cane sugar
2 tablespoons honey
25 g (1 oz) butter
finely grated rind of 1 lemon
½ teaspoon ground cinnamon
3 eggs, separated

Bring the milk to the boil in a heavy-based pan. Sprinkle on the oats and cook gently for 5 minutes, stirring frequently. Beat the sugar, honey, butter, lemon rind and cinnamon into the still warm mixture. Add the beaten egg yolks, one at a time, and mix well.

Stiffly beat the egg whites and fold lightly into the oat mixture. Turn into a greased 1·25-litre (2-pint) pudding basin. Cover with greased, pleated, greaseproof paper and foil and tie securely with string. Steam for 1½ hours. Turn out and serve immediately with warmed golden syrup, honey or jam and single cream. *Serves 6*

Apple and Coriander Crumble

Cooking time 30 minutes

450 g (1 lb) cooking apples
3 tablespoons brown sugar
1 teaspoon ground cinnamon
100 g (4 oz) plain wholemeal flour
50 g (2 oz) butter or margarine
1 teaspoon crushed coriander seeds

Peel the cooking apples and grate into a 1-litre (1½-pint) ovenproof dish. Sprinkle with 1 tablespoon of the sugar and the cinnamon.

Rub the flour and butter together until the mixture resembles fine breadcrumbs. Mix in the remaining sugar. Smooth this mixture on top of the apples then sprinkle with the coriander seeds.

Bake in a moderate oven (180°C, 350°F, Gas Mark 4) for 30 minutes. Serve hot or cold with yogurt or single cream. *Serves 4*

Pear and Apricot Flan

Cooking time 45 minutes

Pastry
150 g (5 oz) plain wholemeal flour
75 g (3 oz) butter, softened
50 g (2 oz) light raw cane sugar
1 egg

Filling
75 g (3 oz) dried apricots
2 tablespoons lemon juice
2 dessert pears, peeled
50 g (2 oz) light raw cane sugar
¼ teaspoon ground cinnamon

Place all the pastry ingredients in a bowl and mix, using a wooden spoon, until the mixture binds together to form a soft dough. Knead lightly until smooth. Wrap in cling film or foil and refrigerate for about 30 minutes.

Place the apricots in a saucepan with 600 ml (1 pint) water and bring to the boil. Remove from the heat and leave to soak for 30 minutes (alternatively, soak the apricots in cold water overnight).

Brush an 18-cm (7-inch) flan ring with a little oil. Roll out the pastry to fit the flan ring, then chill until required.

Place the lemon juice in a saucer and core the pears. Slice thinly and turn in the lemon juice to prevent them from turning brown. Drain the apricots and cut in half. Mix half the sugar with the cinnamon. Place a layer of pear slices on the base of the flan, add half the apricots and sprinkle with the sugar and cinnamon mixture. Cover with the remaining pears and apricots and sprinkle with the remaining sugar.

Bake in the centre of a moderately hot oven (190°C, 375°F, Gas Mark 5) for 40–45 minutes, until the pastry has begun to shrink from the sides of the flan ring. Remove and cool. Serve cold with cream or custard. *Serves 6–8*

Coconut Cream Pie

Cooking time 40 minutes

175 g (6 oz) sweet shortcrust pastry
225 g (8 oz) raw cane sugar
65 g (2½ oz) flour
1 teaspoon salt
750 ml (1¼ pints) lukewarm milk
3 egg yolks
2 tablespoons butter
1 teaspoon vanilla essence
65 g (2½ oz) desiccated coconut

On a lightly floured surface, roll out the pastry to fit a 23-cm (9-inch) pie dish. Gently ease the pastry into the dish and trim and flute the eges. Place on a baking tray.

Prick the base of the pastry case several times, line with foil and sprinkle with dried beans or rice. Bake blind in a moderately hot oven (200°C, 400°F, Gas Mark 6) for about 15 minutes, or until the pastry is golden. Remove from the oven and leave to cool.

Meanwhile prepare the filling. Put the sugar, flour and salt in a medium-sized bowl and mix well. Stirring constantly with a wooden spoon, pour in the lukewarm milk in a steady stream. Cook over a moderate heat for about 10 minutes or until the mixture thickens. Remove from the heat and leave to stand for 5 minutes.

In a small bowl, beat the egg yolks together. Add 3 tablespoons of the thickened milk mixture and mix well. Pour the egg mixture into the remaining thickened milk mixture. Return to the heat and cook, stirring constantly, for a further 3 minutes, or until the mixture is quite thick.

Stir the butter, vanilla essence and all but 2 tablespoons of the coconut into the thick mixture and pile it into the baked pastry case. Sprinkle the remaining coconut on top and bake in the centre of a moderately hot oven (200°C, 400°F, Gas Mark 6) for about 20 minutes or until lightly browned. Leave to cool completely before serving. *Serves 8*

Compote of Figs with Almonds

Cooking time 10–15 minutes

50 g (2 oz) raw cane sugar
150 ml (¼ pint) water
1 vanilla pod
450 g (1 lb) fresh figs, peeled
50 g (2 oz) blanched almonds

Place the sugar, water and vanilla pod in a saucepan and heat gently to dissolve the sugar. Add the whole figs and stew very gently in the vanilla syrup for 10–15 minutes, depending upon their ripeness.

Remove the vanilla pod and stir in the almonds. Chill and serve with single cream. *Serves 4*

Cider Fruit Salad

450 g (1 lb) dried fruit salad
300 ml (½ pint) sweet cider
1 (6-cm/2½-inch) piece cinnamon stick
1 tablespoon lemon juice

Place the dried fruit salad in a medium mixing bowl and pour over the cider (warm the cider if soaking time is short). Leave to soak overnight, or for at least 6 hours, with the cinnamon stick and lemon juice.

Before serving, remove the cinnamon stick and divide between four individual serving dishes. Serve with whipped cream or natural yogurt and sprinkle with toasted hazelnuts. *Serves 4*

Yogurt and Orange Whip

8 medium oranges
2 tablespoons clear honey
600 ml (1 pint) natural yogurt
4 tablespoons chopped walnuts, almonds
or hazelnuts

Peel the oranges, removing as much white pith as possible. Reserve about 2 tablespoons of the orange rind and chop it finely. Set aside.

With a sharp knife, chop the orange flesh into small pieces and place them in a liquidiser. Add the honey and yogurt and liquidise at high speed for about 20 seconds, or until the ingredients are well combined.

Pour the orange mixture into six individual glass serving dishes or stemmed glasses. Place in the refrigerator to chill for at least 2 hours. Just before serving, sprinkle the tops with the nuts and reserved orange rind. *Serves 6*

Frozen Coffee and Almond Yogurt

300 ml (½ pint) home-made yogurt (see
page 67)
2 tablespoons very strong black coffee
2 tablespoons dark raw cane sugar
2 egg whites
50 g (2 oz) flaked almonds, toasted

Pour the yogurt into a mixing bowl. Add the black coffee and sugar and mix well.

Whisk the egg whites until very stiff, then fold into the yogurt mixture with the toasted flaked almonds. Pour into four individual dishes and freeze until firm. Allow to stand in the refrigerator for 30 minutes before serving. *Serves 4*

Brown Bread Ice Cream

150 ml (¼ pint) double cream
1 (142-ml/5-fl oz) carton natural
yogurt
2 eggs, separated
50 g (2 oz) fresh wholemeal
breadcrumbs
1 tablespoon sherry or rum
25 g (1 oz) icing sugar

◇ ● ♥

Beat the double cream until thick. Fold in the yogurt and egg yolks and mix well. Stir in the breadcrumbs and sherry or rum.

Beat the egg whites until stiff and fold in the sifted sugar and the cream mixture. Pour into a freezing tray or container and freeze until firm.

For a smoother ice cream, when the mixture is half frozen, turn out into a bowl and whisk for 2 minutes. Return to the freezer tray and freeze until firm. *Serves 4*

Pear and Honey Sorbet

Cooking time 15 minutes

900 g (2 lb) pears
grated rind and juice of 1 lemon
2–3 tablespoons honey
1 egg white

◇ ○ ♡

Cut the pears into quarters, remove the cores and peel. Slice into a saucepan. Add the lemon rind and juice and the honey.

Cover the pan and cook over a low heat for 15 minutes, or until the pears are tender. Sieve or liquidise to a smooth purée.

Pour the pear purée into a shallow container and freeze for about 1 hour, or until half frozen. Remove from the freezer and beat well. Whisk the egg white until stiff and fold into the purée. Return to the freezer until solid then cover tightly. Store in the freezer for up to 3 months.

To serve, allow the sorbet to soften slightly, then spoon into four individual glasses. *Serves 4*

Baking

Wholemeal Bread
Cooking time 50 minutes plus 2–2¼ hours rising time

1½ teaspoons butter or margarine
25 g (1 oz) fresh yeast
1 teaspoon brown sugar
900 ml (1½ pints) plus 4 teaspoons
lukewarm water
1.4-kg (3 lb) stoneground wholemeal
flour
1 tablespoon salt
2 tablespoons honey
1 tablespoon oil
4 tablespoons cracked wheat (optional)

Grease four 0·5-kg (1-lb) loaf tins with the butter.

Crumble the yeast into a small mixing bowl and mash with the brown sugar. Add 4 teaspoons of the water and cream with the sugar and yeast to form a smooth paste. Set the bowl aside in a warm place for 15–20 minutes, or until the yeast mixture has risen and is frothy.

Put the flour and salt into a warmed mixing bowl. Make a well in the centre of the flour and pour in the yeast mixture, honey, the remaining water and the oil. Using your fingers, gradually draw the flour into the liquid. Mix in all the flour and continue until the dough comes away from the sides of the bowl.

Turn the dough out on to a floured surface and knead for about 10 minutes, reflouring the surface if the dough becomes sticky.

Rinse and dry the mixing bowl and shape the dough into a ball. Return to the mixing bowl and dust the dough with a little flour. Cover the bowl with a clean, damp cloth or cling film. Leave in a warm place for about 1–1½ hours or until the dough has risen and has almost doubled in bulk.

Turn the risen dough on to a floured surface and knead vigorously for 10 minutes. Cut the dough into four pieces and shape into loaves. Place in the loaf tins. Sprinkle each loaf with a little cracked wheat if liked.

Cover the tins with a damp cloth and return to a warm place for 30–45 minutes or until the dough has risen to the top of the tins.

Place the tins in the centre of a very hot oven (240°C, 475°F, Gas Mark 9) and bake for 15 minutes. Lower the oven temperature to hot (220°C, 425°F, Gas Mark 7), put the bread on a lower shelf in the oven, and bake for a further 25–30 minutes.

After the cooking time is complete, remove the bread from the oven, tip the loaves out of the tins and rap the undersides with your knuckles. If the bread sounds hollow, it is cooked. If not, lower the oven temperature to moderately hot (190°C, 375°F, Gas Mark 5), return the loaves to the oven, upside down, and bake for a further 10 minutes. Remove from oven and cool on a rack. *Makes four 450-g (1-lb) loaves, each serving 4*
Note For variation, the loaves may be baked in well greased flower pots, or shaped into cottage loaves on a baking tray. If liked 40 g (1½ oz) bran can be added with extra water for a bran loaf.

Corn Bread

Cooking time 25 minutes

1 teaspoon butter or margarine
165 g (5½ oz) yellow corn meal
100 g (4 oz) flour
2 teaspoons baking powder
1 teaspoon salt
65 g (2½ oz) vegetable fat
250 ml (8 fl oz) milk
1 egg

Using the butter or margarine, lightly grease a 20-cm (8-inch) square baking tin. Sift the corn meal, flour, baking powder and salt into a medium mixing bowl. Add the vegetable fat and cut it into the flour, using a knife, until the fat is in small pieces. Using the fingertips, rub the fat into the flour until it resembles fine breadcrumbs.

Beat the milk and the egg together. Stir into the flour mixture, until the ingredients are well combined.

Turn the mixture into the tin. Bake in a moderately hot oven (200°C, 400°F, Gas Mark 6) for 25 minutes, or until a skewer inserted into the centre comes out clean.

Cut the corn bread into 5-cm (2-inch) squares. Serve at once with butter and honey. *Makes 16*

Onion and Herb Loaf

Cooking time 1 hour plus 2 hours rising time

15 g ($\frac{1}{2}$ oz) fresh yeast
$\frac{1}{2}$ teaspoon sugar
6 tablespoons lukewarm water
6 tablespoons milk
1 tablespoon butter or margarine
275 g (10 oz) plain wholemeal flour
1 teaspoon salt
1 teaspoon finely chopped sage
2 teaspoons finely chopped savory
1 small onion, peeled and minced
1 teaspoon oil

Crumble the yeast into a small mixing bowl and mash in the sugar with a fork. Add 2 tablespoons of the water and cream together to form a smooth paste. Set aside in a warm place for about 15–20 minutes, or until the yeast mixture has risen and is frothy.

Meanwhile, in a small saucepan, scald the milk over a moderate heat (bring to just under boiling point). Remove from the heat, add the butter or margarine and the remaining water. Set aside and leave until lukewarm.

Put the flour and salt into a warmed mixing bowl. Sprinkle over the sage, savory and onion. Make a well in the centre of the flour and pour in the yeast and milk mixtures. Using your fingers or a spatula, draw the flour mixture into the liquid. Continue mixing until all the flour is incorporated and the dough comes away from the sides of the bowl.

Turn out on to a lightly floured surface and knead for 10 minutes, reflouring the surface if the dough becomes sticky.

Form the dough into a ball and return to the washed and dried mixing bowl. Cover with a damp cloth or cling film and leave to prove in a warm place for 1–1$\frac{1}{2}$ hours, or until the dough has risen and doubled in bulk.

Lightly grease a 0·5-kg (1-lb) loaf tin with the oil and set aside.

Turn the dough out on to a lightly floured surface and knead for 8–10 minutes. Form the dough into a loaf and place in the tin. Cover with a damp cloth or cling film and leave to prove for 30–45 minutes, or until the dough has doubled in bulk again.

Place the loaf in the centre of a moderately hot oven

(200°C, 400°F, Gas Mark 6) and bake for 1 hour. Cool on a wire rack. *Makes one 0·5-kg (1-lb) loaf, serving 4–6 people.*

Note Dried herbs may be used in smaller quantities in this recipe, but the aroma will not be as pungent.

Granary Loaf

Cooking time 40 minutes plus 1½ hours rising time

275 g (10 oz) plain wholemeal flour
275 g (10 oz) strong white flour
1 tablespoon salt
15 g (½ oz) butter or margarine
150 g (5 oz) cracked wheat
50 g (2 oz) wheatgerm
15 g (½ oz) fresh yeast
450 ml (¾ pint) tepid water and milk
2 tablespoons powdered malt

Mix the flours and the salt together in a large bowl. Add the fat and rub in until the mixture resembles very fine breadcrumbs. Add 100 g (4 oz) of the cracked wheat and the wheatgerm and mix well.

In a small bowl, cream the yeast with the water and milk until the yeast has dissolved. Make a well in the flour and pour in the yeast liquid. Add the malt and mix to a soft dough.

Turn out on to a lightly floured surface and knead well for 10 minutes. Put the dough in a greased bowl and cover with greased polythene. Leave in a warm place for 45–60 minutes, or until the dough has doubled in size. Knead for a further 3 minutes, divide in half and shape into two round loaves.

Place the loaves on a greased baking tray and sprinkle with the remaining cracked wheat.

Cover the baking tray with greased polythene and leave in a warm place to rise for 20–30 minutes, or until double in size. Remove the polythene and bake in a hot oven (220°C, 425°F, Gas Mark 7) for 15 minutes. Lower the oven temperature to moderately hot (190°C, 375°F, Gas Mark 5) and continue baking for 20–25 minutes.

If the loaves sound hollow when tapped on the base, they are cooked; if not, return to the oven for a further 5 minutes. *Makes 2 small loaves, each serving 4–6 people*

New England Soda Bread

Cooking time 3¾ hours

2 teaspoons oil
100 g (4 oz) stale, crustless bread,
soaked overnight in 350 ml (12 fl oz)
cold water
6 tablespoons molasses or black treacle
1 teaspoon salt
150 g (5 oz) corn meal
150 g (5 oz) rye flour
150 g (5 oz) 100% wholemeal flour
2 teaspoons bicarbonate of soda
6 tablespoons cold water

Brush two 1-litre (1½-pint) round ovenproof moulds or pudding basins with the oil and set aside.

Using the back of a wooden spoon, rub the soaked bread through a fine metal sieve into a mixing bowl. Add the molasses or treacle to the puréed bread and mix well.

In a second mixing bowl, combine the salt, corn meal, rye flour, wholewheat flour and soda.

Make a well in the centre of the dry ingredients. Pour in the water and add the bread and molasses mixture. Stir until all the ingredients are well mixed.

Divide the mixture between the two bowls. Cover securely with greased aluminium foil, and tie tightly with string under the rim of each basin. Steam for 3–3½ hours.

Bake the loaves in their basins in a cool oven (150°C, 300°F, Gas Mark 2) for about 15 minutes. This will remove any excess moisture from the bread. Turn on to a wire rack. Serve warm or cold with lots of butter and honey or cheese. *Makes 2 loaves, each serving 4–6 people*

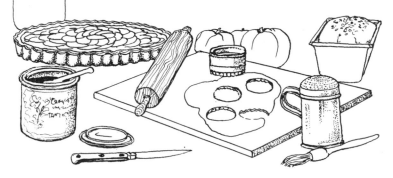

Shortcrust Pastry

225 g (8 oz) plain wholemeal flour
2 teaspoons baking powder
salt
50 g (2 oz) margarine
50 g (2 oz) lard
cold water

Sift the flour, baking powder and salt together into a large mixing bowl. Add any coarse bran left in the sieve. Rub the fats into the flour until the mixture resembles fine breadcrumbs. Bind the mixture together with water – about 2½ tablespoons. Knead lightly to form a stiff dough. Roll out fairly thinly and use as required. *Makes 225 g (8 oz) pastry*

Flaky Pastry

225 g (8 oz) plain wholemeal flour
1 teaspoon salt
2 teaspoons baking powder
75 g (3 oz) margarine
75 g (3 oz) lard
1 teaspoon lemon juice
7–8 tablespoons cold water

Sift the flour, salt and baking powder into a bowl. Work the fats together in another bowl and divide into four. Rub one quarter of the softened fat into the flour and mix to a soft elastic dough with the water and lemon juice.

Roll out the dough to an oblong on a floured board and flake the second quarter of fat over the top two-thirds. Fold the bottom third up and the top third down and give the pastry half a turn, so that the folds are now at the sides. Seal the edges of the pastry by pressing with the rolling pin. Reroll as before, and continue until all the fat is used up. Wrap the pastry loosely in greaseproof paper and leave to rest in the refrigerator for at least 30 minutes before using.

Sprinkle a board or table with very little flour, roll out the pastry to 3 mm (⅛ inch) thick, use as required and bake in a very hot oven (240°C, 475°F, Gas Mark 9). *Makes 225 g (8 oz) pastry*

Harvest Honey Tart

Cooking time 25–35 minutes

Pastry
225 g (8 oz) plain wholemeal flour
100 g (4 oz) margarine
2 tablespoons golden syrup
1 egg

Filling
4 tablespoons clear honey
25 g (1 oz) butter
4 tablespoons mixed cereal with sultanas,
nuts and apple
1 tablespoon light raw cane sugar
225 g (8 oz) Victoria plums
1 large cooking apple

Place the flour in a bowl, add the margarine and rub in until the mixture resembles fine breadcrumbs.

Measure the golden syrup into a basin, add the egg and beat to mix well. Add to the dry ingredients and mix to form a soft dough. Knead lightly until smooth. Cut off one third of the dough for decoration, wrap in cling film or foil and reserve. Roll out the remaining dough to line a 25-cm (10-inch) pie dish. Flute the edges of the pastry.

Roll out the reserved pastry and cut into three long strips. Plait these together and place around the border of the tart. Use any remaining strips to make pastry leaves, harvest mice etc.

Place 3 tablespoons of the honey and the butter in a saucepan and heat until melted. Stir in the mixed cereal and spread over the pastry. Bake in the centre of a moderately hot oven (190°C, 375°F, Gas Mark 5) for 25–35 minutes, until the pastry is golden brown.

Meanwhile, dissolve the sugar in 300 ml ($\frac{1}{2}$ pint) water in a shallow saucepan, and bring to the boil. Cut the plums in half and remove the stones. Peel and core the apples and cut into thick slices. Place these immediately in the boiling syrup. Cook until just tender, remove from the syrup and drain. Add the plums to the pan, cook for 1 minute, then drain. Arrange the plums on the edge of the cereal and the apples in the centre.

Add the last of the honey to the remaining syrup and boil until thick. Remove from the heat and brush over the fruit. Serve with whipped cream or custard. *Serves 6*

Farmhouse Orchard Scones

Cooking time 15–20 minutes

Scones
175 g (6 oz) plain wholemeal flour
50 g (2 oz) plain flour
¼ teaspoon salt
4 teaspoons baking powder
50 g (2 oz) butter
1 egg
4 tablespoons milk
cracked wheat (optional)

Filling
2 tablespoons lemon juice
2 red-skinned apples
100–175 g (4–6 oz) soft cream cheese

Sift the flours, salt and baking powder into a bowl and rub in the butter, until the mixture resembles fine breadcrumbs. Beat the egg and milk together; add to the flour and mix to a soft dough, adding more milk if necessary.

Turn the mixture on to a floured surface and knead lightly until smooth. Mould into a 15-cm (6-inch) round and place on a lightly floured baking tray. Mark into eight wedges with a sharp knife and brush with the milk. Sprinkle the top with cracked wheat if liked.

Bake just above the centre of a hot oven (230°C, 450°F, Gas Mark 8) for about 15–20 minutes, until well risen and firm to the touch. Leave to cool.

Place the lemon juice in a small saucer. Remove the cores from the apples and cut one into eight thick slices. Turn the slices in the lemon juice to prevent them turning brown. Finely chop the remaining apple, add any remaining lemon juice and mix thoroughly with the cream cheese.

To serve, break the scones in half and serve with the filling garnished with the apple slices. *Makes 8*

Sunflower Seed Walnut Bars

Cooking time 45 minutes

350 ml (12 fl oz) oil
350 ml (12 fl oz) honey
6 eggs
4 teaspoons baking powder
675 g (1½ lb) plain wholemeal flour
few drops of vanilla essence
2 tablespoons grated orange rind
4 tablespoons orange juice
50 g (2 oz) shredded, unsweetened coconut
50 g (2 oz) sunflower seeds
50 g (2 oz) walnuts, chopped

To make the bottom layer, mix half the oil, a third of the honey, 2 eggs, 2 teaspoons baking powder, half the flour and the vanilla essence together. Pat into two 23 × 33-cm (9 × 13-inch) greased tins.

For the topping, beat the remaining 4 eggs with the remaining ingredients and pour over the bottom layer. Bake in a moderate oven (160°C, 325°F, Gas Mark 3) for about 45 minutes. Cool and cut into squares. *Makes 18*

Natural Health Candy

225 g (8 oz) dates
450 g (1 lb) dried figs
275 g (10 z) walnuts, chopped
50 g (2 oz) seedless raisins
450 g (1 lb) dried apricots
1 teaspoon grated orange rind, sesame seeds, or shredded, unsweetened coconut

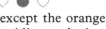

Put all the ingredients except the orange rind, sesame seeds or coconut into a liquidiser and mix well. Press into two 18-cm (7-inch) square shallow, buttered trays. Cut into 2·5-cm (1-inch) squares. Roll in orange rind, seasame seeds or coconut. *Makes 49 pieces*

Index